THE HAPPY BUSINESS REVOLUTION

How to make your business great for you, your team and your customers

Mike Jones

Rethink

First published in Great Britain in 2024
by Rethink Press (www.rethinkpress.com)

This book is dedicated to those exceptional leaders and business pioneers who prove every day that true success comes from elevating others while chasing our goals. Your example lights the path for others to follow.

Contents

Introduction

Since 2018 I've worked with hundreds of employees, business leaders and business owners across a wide range of industries to improve health, happiness and performance in the workplace. I've supported businesses ranging from five or fewer employees to some of the largest employers in the UK. Although the size and structure of the companies I work with varies widely, I encounter the same issues, caused by the same mistakes, which lead to the same struggles.

What I've learned is that for most people, work is more of a stress than a joy. This includes everyone from owners and CEOs to managers and employees. No business owner starts out with the intention of their business being anything other than incredible. We start our businesses with visions of freedom and impact for ourselves; growing teams that love working for us; and delivering a service to customers that blows their socks off.

But something happens along the way. At some point, that excitement and enthusiasm gets overtaken by the inevitable stresses of business. Owners end up feeling more stuck than free; leaders and managers struggle with overwhelm; and employees become demotivated or bored. I understand this not just through working with other businesses, but through painful personal experience.

I served for five years in the British military, including two tours of Afghanistan, and then travelled for three years. While I travelled, I engaged in extensive study of spirituality, especially Buddhism, and lived on monasteries in Nepal and Thailand. When I returned to the UK in 2016, I founded my first business. Bright eyed and totally naïve to the world of business, I opened a group training gym. I didn't have a clear plan. I had no experience. But with a bit of cash and a heart full of excitement I completely believed that I would succeed and that it would be an epic journey.

Within two years, I had enough committed clients to warrant leasing my own unit. Over the next three years we grew to a team of five and doubled our revenue every year until we had a healthy, profitable six-figure business. But while the business was doing great, I wasn't.

Somewhere between years two and three, my excitement had been overtaken by stress. I was working six to seven days per week, early in the morning until late in the evening. My partner and I had taken just two holidays in five years. I paid myself next to nothing and pumped everything back into the business. The only time I really saw my partner was when she was training at the gym, and I remember feeling a deep sense of shame when she asked me if I still wanted to be with her. She told me I always seemed happy at the gym but when I was at home I was tired, disinterested or working on the computer and moody. The truth was I was shattered, but I put the effort in to hide it at the gym because I was at work. My staff knew I was stressed, and the visionary energy I started with had disappeared. The business had gone from an exciting adventure to a stressful burden, and that began to rub off on my team.

By the time COVID-19 came around, I was completely burned out and depressed. Before I had my own business, if I was unhappy or dissatisfied at work there was always someone higher up I could attach blame to. Getting burned out as a business owner meant there was only one person I could point the finger at: myself.

After experiencing burnout for myself, I knew that my purpose was to find a solution that prevents work from becoming unhealthy and makes businesses great for leaders, managers and employees. My experience taught me that to fix the workplace struggle problem, a top–down approach was required. If the business owners/leaders and managers were stressed and on the way to burnout, the experience for the employees would always be poor and the business would never reach its potential.

I founded a company, Better Happy, with the vision of 'every employee happy, every business thriving.' I talked about my experience of burnout and built the tools and systems that would prevent it from happening again. I thought business owners would be interested in what I was sharing, and they were, but what surprised me was the interest that came from other people. It turned out that it's not just business owners who struggle with stress-related overwork but managers and leaders in all sorts of companies. I got opportunities to work with small businesses, medium businesses and some of the largest employers in the UK. With every team I worked with, I obsessed over the same question: what's getting in the way of a win/win situation for everyone?

Before long, I noticed that the teams and businesses I was supporting made the same mistakes, which led to the same issues. I had similar conversations over and over again. Whether I was working with a business owner or a new manager, there were so many similarities:

- 'Do you have a plan for where you're heading?' 'No.'
- 'Do you make time to plan, listen to and develop your team?' 'No.'
- 'Do you prioritise a few goals and track progress towards them?' 'No.'
- 'Do you track numbers that give you a clear indication of the business/team and each person within it?' 'No.'
- 'Do you create a culture of psychological safety where healthy conflict is encouraged?' 'No.'
- 'Do you prioritise yourself and make time for your health?' 'No.'

I probed to see if the people I worked with made the mistakes I had made in my first business and retrospectively learned how to address. Turns out, they're pretty common mistakes. I was soon able to group the issues teams faced into five categories, which led to the creation of the SELPH model:

1. **Strategy:** Is there a simple and clear plan for where you're aiming to be one to ten years from now?
2. **Engagement:** Have you got systems in place to engage with and develop your people so they love working for you and genuinely want your business to succeed?

3. **Leadership:** Does your leadership team function well and drive collaborative growth across all people in the business?
4. **Performance:** Do you have goal-setting and tracking systems in place that drive growth while preventing overcommitment?
5. **Health:** Are you creating a culture of health and vitality in your business where leadership, managers and employees improve their health alongside work?

Using this model, we now help teams and businesses be growth-minded, enjoyable and great places to work. When you implement the SELPH model in your business, it creates a win/win for you and your people. Your business will stop being dependent on the owner. You'll develop a level of employee leadership and motivation other businesses can't fathom. Growing your business will stop feeling like an owner-driven slog as your team begin to do it for you, with enjoyment and on autopilot.

The cynic in you might say 'to really make my people happy, I just need to pay them more.' That's rarely the case. You absolutely need to pay your people enough – and ideally more than enough – but many people aren't highly motivated by money. You can pay your people the best salaries in the world but if you've got a crappy culture, they'll still look elsewhere or just won't enjoy working for you. When you implement the SELPH model, paying people more will become a natural byproduct of your success. As your people become more engaged and your leadership more strategic, your revenue, profits and salaries will increase.

You don't make more money to be happy; when you become happier, you make more money. The most successful businesses of the future will be the ones that passionate people enjoy working in. It doesn't matter what industry you're in or how big your business is, you have the ability to make it a great place to work and to outperform your competitors by doing so. While other businesses struggle to cope with rapid change and the problems it creates, your people and business will revel in change. The SELPH model is your step-by-step guide to make that a reality in your business, but first we need to deal with you: the business owner. We'll do this in Part One of the book, before we move on to the SELPH model in Parts Two and Three.

PART ONE
THE PARADIGM SHIFT

The world we live in is evolving rapidly, creating more change and opportunity than ever before. With the right mindset, you and your people can thrive in this exciting era. With the wrong mindset, you're destined to struggle.

Let's get that mindset right.

ONE
Stressed Owner, Stressed Business

Every business owner has their own unique reasons for choosing to step away from social norms and become a business owner. Although everyone's reasons are different, we can safely assume that for most entrepreneurs we will find a combination of the desire to make a difference, to do meaningful work and to live life on their own terms. Done right, with a bit of good timing and luck, a business will provide the owner and their team(s) with all of those things and more.

Spending just a little bit of time on social media or networking can quickly convince you that most people are nailing it in business. They appear to be having the time of their lives growing their businesses and making money by delighting their customers, with a team that loves working for them. My experience shows me that this isn't true, and the data backs it up.

A 2023 NHS survey of small business owners found that 80% had suffered with poor mental health and 38% with depression.[1] Another study found that 43% of employees feel exhausted.[2] Gallup's famous 'State of the Global Workplace' report consistently shows the UK to have one of the lowest levels of employee engagement in the world. In their 2023 report, our engagement levels came in at 10%.[3] That's a mere 10% of all surveyed employees in the UK that actually enjoy being at work. Of course data can be manipulated to tell the story you want it to, but ask yourself this: how many people do you know, yourself included, who are genuinely happy in their work, who find an enormous sense of satisfaction through their work and for whom work doesn't have a negative impact on their physical or mental health?

In the companies I work with, I encounter the same phenomenon and the same emotional struggles. Most people genuinely care about the company they work for and want to do a good job. They care about the other people in the business and want them to be happy. And from owners and CEOs down to team members, they experience more negative than positive impact on their health and happiness from work.

Those from management level upwards suffer unhealthy levels of stress and an inability to switch off. They do too much and feel pulled between the needs of the business and the needs of their people. Those from team leader downwards suffer frustration that things don't change and resentment because they don't feel appreciated or listened to. The result is that everyone struggles with their health because when the work you do doesn't energise you, there's not much motivation to look after your own health.

What's clear is that most struggles in work come about not through exploitative people taking advantage of others, but through a joint desire to do things well. The problem isn't with the people but the vehicle. We are hardwired to want to do good work that contributes to society and to want to have fulfilling relationships. This means we have all the raw ingredients to create a win/win happy work culture where growth is an enjoyable team journey, not a lonely uphill battle. Throughout this book, I'm going to show you exactly how to build the vehicle that enables that. But first, we have to get clear on what might get in your way, by working out what kind of business owner you are.

The three types of business owner

Not all business owners are created equal. Although they share a common set of traits, such as being future- and goal-driven, the way in which they think and operate varies. From working with a variety of business owners, I've recognised that they fall into three broad categories. By knowing generally which category you fall into, you will be able to overcome issues faster or avoid them completely so that you, your team and your business can be better and faster.

The three types of business owner are:

1. **Profit-driven**: Driven by financial success
2. **Purpose-driven**: Driven by the desire to make a difference
3. **People-driven**: Driven by the desire to help people

You might identify strongly with just one or feel like you are a mix of two or more, but you will lead with one. My experience shows me that it's the people- and purpose-driven owners that get stuck for the longest in business. The profit-driven entrepreneurs are super clear on what they want and how they are going to get it. Whether you like them or not, they're efficient and the people who work for them not only get paid well, but know exactly what is expected of them.

People- and purpose-driven owners can get trapped both through a lack of clarity on what it is they actually want and by trying to keep everyone 'happy'. But with the right tools and mindset, the people- and purpose-driven entrepreneurs have more potential for long-term growth and impact through their businesses. Considering that you're reading a book with this title, it seems to me that you're most likely a primarily people- or purpose-driven entrepreneur (my apologies to any profit-driven friends who are reading).

Discovering the Core Four will help you ensure your business is a win/win for everyone involved, including yourself, regardless of your owner type.

The Core Four model

My own experience of business ownership and burnout led to the development of the Core Four model. This simple model changes how people think about and run their businesses, enabling them to create win/win cultures that people – including the owner – love to be a part of.

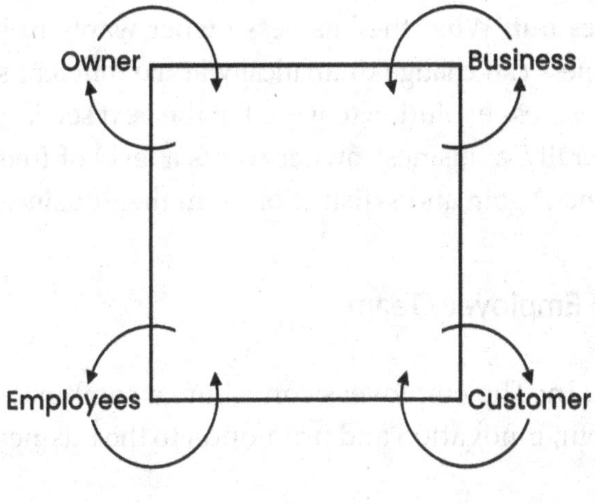

The wording of the Core Four changes slightly once a company has a board, but the principles remain the same. The model shows what each of the 'core four' components put into a business, and what they take out. Getting to grips with this model will help you keep clear in your mind what your business represents to and how it serves different people before you begin your journey with implementing the SELPH model. For this book, we will use the model of a privately owned business without a board.

The Owner

Puts in: The owner is the heart of the business, even after it is sold. You conceive the idea of the business and create the vision. You put in funds and often work for little or nothing in the early stages. As the business grows, you continue to inspire and motivate the workforce through your leadership.

Takes out: What the business owner wants from the business can change dramatically at the different stages of business evolution (covered in the next section), but generally, a business owner wants a level of freedom, financial gain and satisfaction from their business.

The Employee/Team

Puts in: The employees contribute a combination of labour, innovation and promotion to the business. As we'll learn shortly, there is a decreasing value placed on labour and increasing value on innovation.

Takes out: In return for their work, the employee expects the basics of fair pay, good working conditions and an acceptable work–life balance. But it's important to note that in line with increasing quality of life, employees now are looking for more than just the basics. They also want purpose, growth, values alignment and meaningful relationships. We'll cover this in more depth later in this chapter and in detail in the engagement chapter of Part Two.

The Customer

Puts in: In simple terms, the customer puts in money and referrals to the business.

Takes out: In return for money, the customer expects value. They receive this through a combination of services or products that solve a problem or feed a desire.

The Business

Note – it might seem strange, but it's extremely useful to think of the business itself as a person.

Puts in: The business provides structure and validity, a legal medium through which the other relationships can be served.

Takes out: A business wants and needs profit. Although a business can survive without it, it won't prosper long term or be an enjoyable place to work if it can't turn a profit.

I want you to look at your business through the lens of the Core Four. Are those relationships harmonious or dysfunctional? You will be able to identify the root cause of most issues in your business by breaking it down like this.

For example, looking back on my first business through this lens I can see that my obsession with pleasing customers damaged the rest of the business. I wanted to provide the best service possible but resisted putting prices up in order to keep customers happy. This meant I had to work crazy hours and my fantastic team wasn't getting paid the salaries they deserved.

Tommy Mello, the owner of A1 Garage Doors in the USA, sums up this common situation well in his book *Elevate*. A1 Garage Doors now has a huge team and turns over $100m per year, but it wasn't too long ago that it was a small and struggling company. Mello accepted that something had to change when he began stealing toilet rolls from his own facility to get by. The realisation that ultimately transformed his business was that he wasn't charging enough to provide a quality service or pay people well. As he puts it, 'I was screwing my team and business to look after my customers.'[4]

The business owner blinded by their pursuit of profit might screw their team and customers to drive up profits. This works for the owner and the business in the short term but as the team and customers get fed up, issues will follow. It can't be avoided – an enjoyable and successful business has to support all of the Core Four in the ecosystem.

Remember, the owner is 25% of the Core Four. As the owner of the business, its future success and the fulfilment of your employees is heavily dependent upon you – no pressure. Keeping yourself focused and motivated isn't as difficult as you might think; you just have to be as clear on what *you* want from the business as you are on your customers and team. If you're not entirely sure, then understanding the Four Stages of Growth will help.

The Four Stages of Growth

When you have the entrepreneurial spirit, you will only be happy when you're involved in business. But this can also make you feel trapped. A trapped entrepreneur is an unhappy entrepreneur. Getting stuck in this way is what led to me burning out, and working with so many other business owners made it clear to me just how widespread this problem is.

This problem is both avoidable and solvable. I created the Four Stages of Growth map to help you avoid getting trapped and demotivated in your businesses. It is essential that you avoid this trap because you can't have a happy business without a happy leader.

A key principle I teach to the business owners and their teams that work with us is to be sensibly selfish – to prioritise and take good care of yourself so that you can be of most value to others. This is important for everyone in life but especially so for business owners. Your ideas, determination and drive are what you were put on this planet to pursue. When you pursue these things, you create new opportunities that benefit the lives of others.

To be sensibly selfish you have to do a lot of what you love and little of what you dislike. Most business owners love to pursue ideas and bring new things into reality. That's why you can do what most people never could: get a business started. But your business can, and likely will, lead you into a common but predictable trap. When you get stuck there for too long, your ability to be sensibly selfish dissipates. The horrible thing about this trap is that you can't see that you're in it.

You experience the symptoms of being ensnared – you feel stuck, demotivated, your enthusiasm and excitement wanes – but you don't understand why. The trap is of course the business itself. It's the thing that you created, and that's why you can't see it. Because it's what you wanted, you can't understand why you feel this way.

You experience this because what you want and need from the business will change as you and the business grow. These changes occur at a deeper level of consciousness, which is why you experience the symptoms of not feeling fulfilled but don't necessarily understand why. If you have the entrepreneurial spirit, you will only be happy when you pursue growth through business. It's who you are. But feeling stuck in your business will always lead to unhappiness.

The following map will enable you to navigate the journey of growing your business without getting stuck in this trap, enabling you to enjoy the process and be the motivational leader you are meant to be.

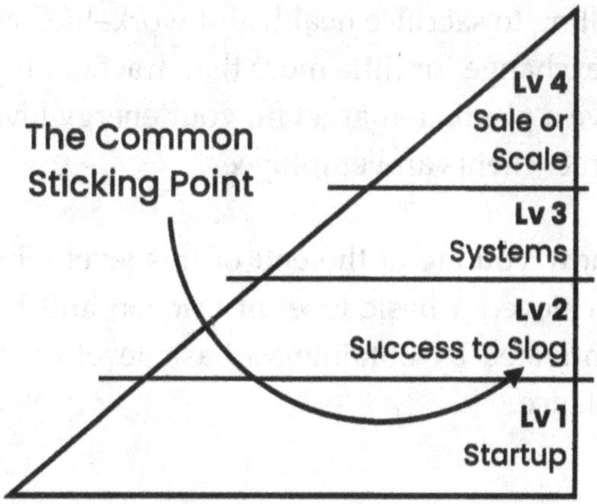

There are four levels in the map. Although I provide rudimentary time frames for each level, these serve as just general guidance. The only true way you will know when you are ready to progress to the next level is when you start to feel unfulfilled or less motivated over an extended period of time (a few weeks or longer). The drop in motivation and lack of fulfilment is your mind's way of telling you it's time to push into new territory – it's acting as a guidance system and warning bell. But if you ignore it for too long, it will actively begin to make you unhealthy and miserable.

Level 1: Startup

The Startup level lasts on average six to twelve months, but can go on longer. In this stage, the owner is:

- Highly motivated by the idea of being their own boss and bringing their vision from concept to reality.
- Willing to sacrifice health and work–life balance in exchange for little more than traction. If you have a product–market fit, your energy levels attract clients and employees.

You know you are at the end of this level when you have achieved a basic level of traction and begin to feel motivated by obtaining a basic level of stability and balance.

Level 2: Success to Slog

The Success to Slog level can last anywhere from two to ten or more years. The tell-tale signs of this stage are:

- A steady base of happy customers and usually a small to medium size team (five to fifty employees).
- People get paid, customers are happy and, initially, so are the owner and team.
- The business and team are heavily reliant on the owner and, although the owner and team enjoy this at the start, as time goes on this can change.

This stage is the sticking point. Eventually, the owner begins to feel constrained by the business and the team constrained by the owner. This should tell all parties involved that it's time to move to the next level.

At the beginning of this stage, everyone has a feeling of winning. Things are working and the work you do makes a difference. Some business owners are genuinely happy at this level for years. You will know that you are reaching the end of this level when success starts to feel like a slog. This happens because business owners usually crave freedom and that's the very reason they start businesses. So, when the business starts to feel 'stagnant' you no longer feel like you are moving towards freedom. You feel like you've created the very thing your business was supposed to help you escape, a job. This is the trap I referred to earlier. Getting stuck here for too long makes you and your team miserable.

Because you have stability at this level, fear will loudly try to talk you out of making any changes. When I work with business owners who face this challenge, the following question always helps put things into context:

> 'Where will you be and how will you feel in two years if you don't change anything?'

If you don't like the answer you come up with, the only thing you truly have to fear is not changing anything. Moving to the next level is the answer to your problems.

Level 3: Systems

To go from an owner-dependent business to a team-run win/win business you have to move to the level of Systems. They may not excite many business owners, but they benefit all of the Core Four.

Moving to the Systems level will:

- Free the business owner from the repetitive aspects of the business so that you can focus on leadership, ideas and decision making.
- Empower the team to deliver a repeatable service/product as well as make decisions and grow the business.

- Create a more consistent experience for customers and lay the groundwork for a business that can scale.
- Significantly increase the value of the business.

Moving to this level is initially uncomfortable for business owners but it pays off quickly. As the systems start to empower the team and deliver a more consistent service to clients, the owner begins to feel genuinely free. This freedom allows the owner to return to spending more time on what they are good at: ideas, learning, mentorship and leadership.

Level 4: Sale or Scale

Once you have systemised your business, it will naturally open itself up to being sold or scaled. That's a decision that you will have to make at some point, but is worth thinking about now. Knowing yourself, your team and the true motivations behind your business will help you make the right decisions at this level. If you are:

- Mainly purpose-driven, you might want to franchise or licence to reach as many people as possible.
- Mainly people-driven, you might want to explore employee ownership or do something similar to the purpose-driven owner.

- Mainly profit-driven, you'll likely have a clear number you want to sell the business for.

What's important to note is that you can't reactively move through the levels. You can't, for example, after getting fed up with being at the Slog level, skip Systemise and jump to Sale. It's going to take you at least two years to get good systems in place so if you're stuck in Slog, start working on the Systems level stuff now. If you hate systems, work with someone who can help you implement.

SYSTEMS DEEP DIVE: Andrew's story

Andrew is the owner of a tooling business. When I started working with Andrew, his main focus was to give his leadership team the tools and support they needed to get results without burning themselves out. He cared deeply about his team and worried about how much they worked. But as we dug deeper, it became clear that he also wanted to work less himself and enjoy a life without the responsibility of the business. It became evident very quickly that what Andrew and his team needed were systems. A lack of systems based on Andrew's way of doing things meant he was stuck in the business and the team were inefficient due to their reliance on him.

Working together, we built systems for the leadership team that supported goal-setting, budget tracking, decision making, goal prioritisation, personal development and work–life balance. Six months later, both the leadership team and Andrew had transformed.

As these systems replaced much of what Andrew did, he was able to work less and do more of what he loved, such as coaching his leadership team and coming up with new ideas. As all of this happened, business performance increased.

Summary

Your purpose as an entrepreneur is to bring ideas into reality. Your unique combination of vision, drive, hard work and willingness to delay gratification means you achieve things the majority of the population can't fathom. Everybody wins when entrepreneurs are enjoying doing what they are meant to do. You benefit people's lives by creating problems to solutions, you create meaningful employment for people and make a positive contribution to the economy.

The lessons of this chapter will enable you to continue to be a purpose-driven, people-driven or profit-driven entrepreneur without getting stuck and miserable. We have identified the most common sticking points for business owners, why they happen and how to overcome or completely avoid them so that you can be happy doing what you do best.

In the next chapter, we'll find out what the true value your business provides to your current and future employees is, beyond money. By understanding what your employees really need and what your business can provide, employee motivation and retention will never be a challenge again. You'll see that your business is perfectly positioned to give the modern employee what they desperately crave: happiness.

TWO

The Modern Business Happiness Opportunity

To take full advantage of this book, you have to think differently. When you think the same as everyone else, you get the same results as everyone else. The reason that most businesses struggle to create cultures that people enjoy being a part of is because the people who lead them think about 'work' in the wrong way. The common view is to see employee engagement and wellbeing as a challenge to overcome: work and business are regarded as stressful things we have to do to get by or to achieve our goals.

In this chapter I'll show you a new way of thinking about business and work, and how it affects the people that are involved. That includes you. I'm going to show you how your own and your employees' happiness is an opportunity to be grasped, not a barrier to be surmounted. When you see your business through this new lens, you will transform how you and your team experience work. Work will shift from an uphill struggle to a rewarding and enjoyable team journey that adds meaning to people's lives.

Without gaining these insights, you run the risk of staying in the same boat as everyone else. You will continue to:

- See work as a necessary burden people must carry in order to achieve goals
- See employee health and engagement as an ongoing battle between the needs of your people and the needs of your business
- Believe that being a small or medium business is a disadvantage when it comes to employee health and engagement

After reading this chapter, you will see how enjoyable the business journey can be and how vital a role your business plays in the health and happiness of your people. You will be ready to lay the foundations that enable both you and your team to truly enjoy the journey towards achieving your business goals.

Employees want comfort but need happiness

As a business owner, you become the expert at spinning lots of plates. You have a lot to think about and many decisions to make. When you're not careful, mental fatigue combined with decision fatigue can make you and those around you unhappy. Mental fatigue can lead to you being snappy and impatient. Decision fatigue can make it seem to others like you don't care. Both damage your self-esteem.

If you're a people-driven or highly empathetic business owner, you will think a lot about your people. Caring for and supporting your people should be something that gives you a deep sense of fulfilment and one of the most rewarding aspects of business ownership. But when that thinking turns to chronic worry, you enter into a difficult situation where your kindness and compassion become exhausting for you and damaging to the business.

It's not surprising that business owners and leaders spend a lot of time worrying about their people. Although our lives are more comfortable and safer than ever before, it doesn't feel that way because we're bombarded with constant messaging telling us how bad everything is. Poor mental and physical health, an obesity epidemic, wars, recession – the list goes on.

The most valuable thing you bring to your business is your personality and mental energy. It's vital that you look after that and don't let your empathy work against you. To do that, you have to change the way you think about your people. You have to understand that what your people need and what your business can provide is happiness, not comfort. I'm not suggesting that you should remove your office chairs and make your people stand on broken glass. What I mean by comfort is the state of sameness that people gravitate towards in order to avoid anything new, anything growth-focused. Your people won't resist the new because of laziness but due to fear and a lack of self-belief. Your caring nature will lead to you to want to provide your people with comfort, but doing so will only create negative results for you, your team and the business.

One of the most common challenges I see among the business owners and leaders I work with is that, by giving people what they crave for in the short term – comfort – a culture of apathy and disengagement arises. Surveys suggest that, on average, between 43% and 53% of employees are bored at work, and 33% of people wanting to leave their jobs cite boredom as the main reason.[5] Empathetic owners that hold out on growth-focused ideas in order to keep things comfortable for their teams end up scratching their heads wondering why people aren't motivated and why they leave for jobs elsewhere.

I had to go on my own spiritual journey to understand the link between growth and true happiness. In my mid-twenties I served in the British military. I was well paid, had limited outgoings, could pretty much buy what I wanted and was respected by my peers. I had a beautiful girlfriend and my family were proud of me. But I was unhappy. Not depressed; I just felt like my life was empty. I didn't understand it at the time, but I was unfulfilled. I was materially happy but spiritually empty.

I couldn't shake the deep feeling that my life wasn't right; that I wasn't making the best use of my time; that there was something more to life. Eventually, I left the military and headed to Southeast Asia. I spent the next two and a half years travelling. I lived with monks in monasteries in Nepal and on the borders of Thailand. I studied Buddhism and spirituality. I lived with communities that have less than us but who were genuinely happier. I meditated.

I learned many things about myself and the world during that time that changed my life forever, but the one key lesson was this: the meaning of life is happiness. We all want happiness, but in the Western world we don't understand what it is. We've been conditioned to believe that happiness is a combination of comfort, sensual pleasure and material satisfaction. In the UK, we've created more of that for ourselves than ever before in human history. The result? Rising levels of poor physical health and stress-related sickness. In

1993, 14.9% of UK adults were classified as obese. In 2023, that number increased to 25.9%.[6]

True happiness, as I have learned, is the deep sense of fulfilment found by using one's unique strengths to help others. True happiness is found through a combination of personal development, meaningful work and meaningful relationships. Modern society isn't configured to make people truly happy. It is designed to profit by giving people more of what they want. It encourages people to be comfortable but unhappy. People need a reason to be better and support to be the best version of themselves, to be happy.

In a world of comfort and luxury, one of the last places this happens is in the workplace. As a business owner or leader your role isn't to keep your people comfortable. Your job is to help them become the best version of themselves so that they, their teams and your business can grow together. The businesses that get this create cultures of health, happiness and high performance that people flock to. The leaders in the businesses that don't are left scratching their heads wondering why they struggle to find new employees and motivate their existing ones.

The win/win of business and happiness

If you went back in time to 1920s Britain, you'd find a very different world to the one of today; one where:

- Mass unemployment was high
- Quality of living was poor – just getting by was hard
- Most work was product-based manual labour
- The ball was in the employer's court, which often meant terrible working conditions
- Business innovation was slow

Today, the picture looks better:

- In May 2022, the BBC reported that, for the first time since records began, there were more job vacancies than unemployed people.[7]
- Quality of living is comparatively high.
- Work is increasingly creative and service-based.
- The ball is in the workers' court – employers have to support and take care of employees.
- In any industry, change is constant and rapid.

Although these changes have lots of ramifications, they create two important shifts that business owners and leaders must understand.

First, what is needed from employees has changed. A hundred years ago, all you needed was people to follow instructions. Today, you need engaged employees that genuinely care about the success of the company.

Second, the psychology of the employee and what they want from work has changed. Before, people were desperate for work to escape poverty and survive. Today, an increasing number of people aren't working because they have to but because they want to. We will cover why this is in more detail in the engagement chapter of Part Two.

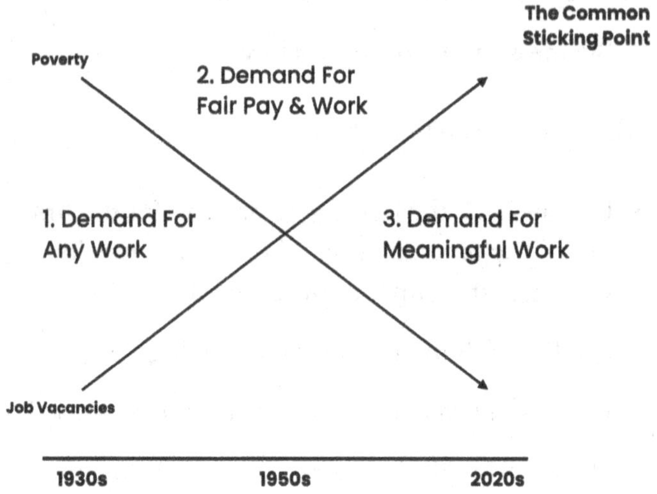

In essence, modern employees are no longer willing to transactionally trade time for money. They work because they want to, not because they have to, and they have a wide range of work available to them. People work not only to get paid, but also to grow and experience fulfilment in life. They work, subconsciously, to improve their happiness.

Survival is still part of people's motivation for working but it's no longer the primary driving force.

Understanding this is essential because it enables you to see what the majority of business leaders do not: the changing psychology of the employee is perfectly aligned to the changing needs of business. If you organise your business to meet the needs of the new employee psychology, they will go above and beyond to make your company a success. If you think that's only true in companies that are trying to change the world, you're wrong. You don't need to be the Red Cross to provide meaningful work, meaningful relationships and the opportunity to grow.

I've seen the power of this approach work in accountancy firms, cleaning companies, hospitality and more. It works because businesses make a difference to people and, no matter how small you might think that difference is, it is enough to give your employees an enormous sense of meaning and a reason to grow.

Most businesses act like video rental giant Blockbuster did in reaction to the advent of the internet and online streaming. Instead of embracing technology, Blockbuster focused on doing what they had always done – renting videos and DVDs – because that's what had worked for them in the past. Blockbuster is no more. Their mistake was seeing themselves as a video rental company when what they actually were was a digital media rental company. Had they seen themselves this way, they would have adapted to the new environment and, by using the traction they already had in the market, potentially still be a leader in the market today.

Most businesses still view themselves as merely providers of products/services for customers and a way for employees to earn money. They're being Blockbuster in response to streaming. You have the opportunity to stand out and be different. You aren't a provider of services/products and paid work; you are a provider of:

- Meaning and purpose
- A shared community where people work together towards a common purpose
- An environment for personal and professional development

You are the provider of everything required for people to connect and improve their happiness in the busy modern world. By understanding that your employees are subconsciously searching for happiness and that your business is the perfect vehicle to find it, you set your business and people up to thrive where most are struggling. In Parts Two and Three of this book, I'll show you exactly how to do that.

The last bastion of happiness

For those of us fortunate enough to be born into developed countries not involved in major conflict, life today is good. Although we still have challenges, we also have more freedom, opportunity, safety and security than ever before.

Yet people also seem to be more generally unhealthy and unhappy than ever before. Poor physical health, mental health and low levels of motivation are not just modern business problems but modern *life* problems. The comfort and security our ancestors worked tirelessly to provide us with does not automatically equate to happiness. Happiness is not merely the absence of struggle. Quite the opposite, as it turns out. Without meaningful struggle, without a reason to unite with others and work collectively towards a common goal, we become unhappy. No matter how comfortable we make life or how much pleasure we have available to us, life without goals and teamwork is unfulfilling at best and depressing at worst.

For most of human history, the daily lives of all humans on earth have been filled, in some form or another, with the pursuit of activities that enable survival. Although this idea may feel distant for many of us in positions of material privilege, it's still true for millions of people today.

In the past, the average person in the UK worked in awful conditions. George Orwell gives a detailed insight into the bleak lives of working-class British people in his 1937 book *The Road to Wigan Pier*.[8] Work was a means to remove a family from poverty and, as such, terrible working conditions didn't seem so terrible. Quality of life was tough, but the toughness of life was a shared struggle that united families and communities. It brought people together. It's also important to note that, back then, it was normal to attend church, which enabled people to find spiritual meaning in life and connection to others through religion. Overall, although life was significantly harder than today, people were closer and arguably less depressed.

Fast forward to today, and not only have we removed much of the daily struggle from life but we are now drastically altering our environment to provide luxury and pleasure. We are constantly seeking to make it quicker, easier and more affordable for people to get what they want. Previous generations would be amazed at what we now take for granted, but gobsmacked at the epidemic of poor physical and mental health that exists in spite of major health improvements and advances in technology.

There is a concept I learned from listening to Jim Rohn's audio series *The Art of Exceptional Living*[9] that will serve you well as a leader: You can solve all of your problems and still not have what you want. Getting rid of the bad stuff in life does not automatically lead to getting the good stuff. If we want the good stuff, we have to prioritise it and work hard to achieve it. Our ancestors' lives were largely dictated by removing life-threatening issues. Today, our focus does not need to be on survival, on removing the bad stuff – it should be on how to thrive and be happy.

Happy humans need meaning, connection and personal growth. The new environment in which we live enables all of this but it doesn't automatically encourage it. Religion does encourage this, but as people increasingly prefer to put their faith in science and rationality, religion is becoming less popular. People in developed wealthy countries are living in an environment where they have the freedom and opportunity to either live the best lives humans have ever had or the laziest and most depressing.

What we need in order to take advantage of the new environment and not let it take advantage of us is: meaning, connection and personal growth. People can find these through the work you make available to them. You have the power, through your business, to provide people with this. The modern business gives the modern human all the ingredients necessary to be truly happy and to thrive in this environment of abundance that has been gifted to us. Businesses are a vital part of the solution to our modern malaise.

Removing the money barrier

Reading this chapter, you might feel a sense of clarity and motivation rising within you, excitement about how great your business can be for all involved, only to be held back by a nagging voice that says 'not in our industry,' 'not in our business,' or 'maybe for other businesses, but not ours.' This voice will be particularly loud if you feel that you are in an industry where it's difficult to be well paid. This is exactly how I felt about my first business in the fitness industry. But since founding Better Happy, I've realised it's an issue that business owners in *all* industries struggle with. It's actually an owner mindset issue, not an industry one. Before we go any further, let's address it.

For your business to be a win/win that you, your team and your customers enjoy being a part of, it's going to need to make good money. Don't mistake this as meaning you have to pay people lots of money to be a great place to work. Everyone needs money, but not everyone is highly motivated by it. The proof of this is all around you. If people were only driven by money, we wouldn't have teachers, police or an NHS.

But no matter how great a place you are to work in, if your people are worried about paying the bills, this will affect their happiness and their performance at work. If another employer has a similar culture and offers a more attractive wage, you risk losing good people.

If you're not able to pay your people attractive wages, you're probably undercharging. This is likely because you are basing your pricing on industry averages and competitors. Remember: if you think like everyone else, you will struggle like everyone else.

When I was three years into owning my first business, I knew from looking at the numbers that the model I was using couldn't work. I *couldn't* make enough money to pay my coaches the wage they deserved without ramming more people into our sessions. If we did that, the quality we were so proud of would drop. My mentor at the time told me the obvious solution: 'You need to charge more – a lot more.' At the time, this felt like the most difficult decision in the world. We changed our prices from a maximum of £80 to a minimum of £150 and a maximum of £400. I was sure there would be a mass walkout and the business would implode. A few clients left but, over the next three months, we hit record levels of new members. We had the money to pay our staff well and constantly improve the facility. Everybody won and at least half of the people who'd left, came back.

For a small or medium business to be a win/win happy place to work, you have to have high prices and a high-quality service level. If you try to be the cheapest, you'll get crushed by bigger companies with more leverage and probably hate what you do. If you price the same as everyone else, you'll struggle to stand out and make money. But if you deliver a premium service and get customers better results, you will find it easy to attract customers who are willing to pay more and, in turn, be able to attract and hold onto motivated employees.

Summary

Running a business is a complex operation that constantly pulls your attention in multiple directions. It should and can be a rewarding challenge that contributes to your life in a variety of ways. Creating work for others through your ideas is a gift to the world. By embracing the learnings of Part One of this book, you will be able to enjoy the journey and not get sucked into feeling constantly worried about your people but instead excited by what your business can do for them. In Part Two, we are going to jump into exactly how you can do this.

PART TWO

THE SELPH METHOD

Your business needs people. The happier your people are, the better and more enjoyable the growth of your business will be.

As we learned in Part One, modern life doesn't make it hard for people to be healthy and happy; it makes it easier for them to be unhealthy and unhappy. Your business is perfectly positioned to address this and the Better Happy SELPH method will show you how.

The five steps of the SELPH model are:

1. Strategy: Communicating your long-term goals and how to get there

Your strategy is everything you have in place to guide your business towards its long-term goals. Typically, in most small and medium businesses, this 'everything' exists only in the owner's head.

Translating an owner's ideas into a documented strategy is essential for the healthy and enjoyable growth of a business. It removes the owner as a bottleneck, reduces the demand on them and enables team-led decision making.

Once you have a formal strategy in place your business instantly begins to feel more fun. The weight of responsibility is lifted from your shoulders and your team is excited for the future. As an added bonus, your clear strategy will open up new opportunities for investment and partnerships.

2. Engagement: Creating an environment in which people love to work and are excited to grow your business

Your business needs people. If you create an engaging environment, you will attract and retain great people that love helping to grow your business.

When you don't make your workplace engaging, the people aspect of your business feels like a constant uphill battle. You struggle to find employees. You struggle to hold onto the employees you do have and they are either working so hard they're getting burned out or just don't seem interested.

Engagement isn't difficult or complicated. It doesn't require fancy software or large investments, just new ways of thinking and acting. Shifting to an engaging workplace can feel uncomfortable but you will be kicking yourself for not doing it sooner. You will free up your own time and your team will become happier, more confident and more independent. Your business will grow.

3. Leadership: Develop a win/win leadership team

Setting your leadership team up in the right way will make your life better, the business stronger and enable a fantastic culture that lasts. The right leadership team will grow your business more than you can alone.

Today, most leadership teams are not set up for success. Modern society has created an underlying message that conflict or disagreement of any type is bad. When leadership teams avoid confrontation and don't hold each other accountable, a culture of resentment, gossiping and lack of motivation follows. Owners feel like they will never be able to step away because whenever they do, growth stops and issues arise.

Implementing the right strategy with your existing or future leadership team will lay the ground for the holy grail of you working less while the business performs better.

4. Performance: Embed systems that reward growth without burnout

Relying on people's goodwill to grow your business is a mistake. For the good of your people and the good of your business, you need embedded systems for setting and pursuing goals.

Without a solid goal-setting and accountability system, you and your people won't know what the priorities are. With no priorities, everything feels important – and when everything feels important, nothing is important. This creates a culture where people are constantly stressed, trying to do everything at once and frustrated at the lack of meaningful progress being made.

By getting your goal-setting system right, you pave the way for an environment of fulfilling growth without overwhelm. You'll get better results while enjoying the journey, leaving your competitors and their employees scratching their heads.

5. Health

In Part Three, we'll cover what health actually is, how being healthy isn't as hard as you might think and exactly what you need to do to create great health not only for yourself but also your team.

THREE

Strategy

Every business – big, small; young, old – has a strategy. Whether you think you do or not, if you are achieving things, you have some form of strategy. The quality of your strategy influences both the performance of the business and the experience of people involved with the business – from customer to employee to owner. Although a good strategy can't guarantee success, due to unforeseen and unknown circumstances, it significantly increases the odds of success. A good strategy, well executed, can guarantee:

- An engaging working environment
- An empowered team

- A collaborative environment where people enjoy working together
- A freed-up business owner and / or leadership team

In this chapter, we will explore exactly what is meant by strategy and how you can implement a powerful strategy in your business regardless of its size, industry or age. By implementing the lessons of this chapter, you and your people will experience positive changes in not only your professional lives but your personal lives too.

When you ignore strategy and don't fully understand how it works, you run the risk of your business becoming inefficient and stressful. One of the most game-changing gifts you can give to your team, one that will enable you to outperform all of your competition, is permission to focus on what's important and ignore what's not. A good strategy will do this, whereas a poor one will always result in inefficient busyness.

As a business owner, it can feel like creating a clear strategy is the bane of your life. You have clarity in your mind about who you are, what you want to achieve and what you need to do to achieve success, but when it comes to condensing that into a clear and simple format you get stuck. If that's you, fear not. By the end of this chapter, you'll have the blueprint to get it done in no time.

What is strategy?

The Oxford Dictionary definition of strategy is 'a plan, scheme, or course of action designed to achieve a particular objective, especially a long-term or overall aim.'[10] In line with this definition, as part of the SELPH method we coach that strategy is any planning for one year or more into the future. Any planning that happens under one year is typically done in 12-week blocks or 'quarters' and falls under the performance step of the SELPH method.

It's difficult to plan your quarters or manage your time effectively if you don't have a longer-term plan. I often work with business owners and managers who are worried about how much their teams are working and the risk of burnout. They commonly ask for a combination of both time and stress-management coaching to address the situation. My response is to ask about the long-term strategy being worked towards and mostly, the answer is that they have none. It's impossible to prioritise without a strategy, and when you can't prioritise then you end up with a never-ending to-do list.

When I served as an intelligence analyst we categorised intelligence in a particular way, and this has stuck with me when it comes to planning in life and business. Strategic and operational intelligence relates to longer-term planning around the area you are looking to get involved in and how you will operate. As a business owner or leader, this means spending time understanding the market, being clear on what makes you unique and setting one-year-plus goals. Tactical intelligence, on the other hand, is about planning how you operate day to day; how you react to live situations in order to fulfil the strategic and operational goals. The challenge for most business owners is shifting from spending more time on tactics than strategy, to the other way around.

The journey through the jungle

Think of your business as being on a journey through a dense jungle. Your role as the owner is to communicate that journey in a way that excites both customers and employees so that they will join you. How you do this changes as your business grows and you develop as an owner. For example, when you were in the startup phase, you may have attracted people by cutting your way through the jungle yourself and shouting about the exciting destination you were on the way to. People could see you making progress and were excited to follow you.

As people join you, your motivation increases. Now you are entering the success phase. But as the team and demand grows, you start to tire from doing all the cutting and showing your team how to cut too. Team motivation also wanes as they want to do more but feel unable to because they need your guidance but you're so busy cutting the path yourself. This is when the success phase start to feels like a slog. Part of your mind is telling you to carry on cutting because it's got you this far, but 'what got you here won't get you there.' Carry on hacking away at this stage and both you and your team will cease to enjoy the journey.

It's at this point that you have to change your approach from a tactical leader to a strategic leader. You need to stop chopping away at the dense bush of the jungle to spend more time planning and empowering. Now you need to climb the trees to orientate yourself in line with your intended destination and plot a more efficient route towards it. Remind yourself why the ultimate destination is so important and create a simple map. Use this map to consistently remind your team of where they are heading, this will keep them – and you – motivated and on track.

As your team grows and a leadership team shines through, periodically invite them to climb the trees with you. As they work alongside you and learn from past experiences, they will help to create a more detailed map of what they think is the most efficient route towards the end goal. This new map allows for more efficiency, empowerment and motivation throughout the entire team. It frees you up from the daily grind to do more of what you love, such as visioning and mentorship. Your leadership team can plan and make decisions without relying on you. The rest of your employees are crystal clear on not only where they are heading in the long term, but on the key goals they are working towards over the next months and year. With the map you and your leadership team have given them, they can contribute their own ideas on how efficiency can be improved based on the tactical intelligence they gather through day-to-day operations, such as which trees to cut and which to avoid. This gives your employees a deep sense of fulfilment.

As you can see from this analogy, giving yourself permission to step back from the day-to-day and become more strategic is the essential first step to make your business a happy win/win environment for everyone. Let's now find out *how* to do this.

Strategy Map and Long-Range Planner

Data suggests that up to 65% of SMEs don't have business plans.[11] While that might seem shocking, it just confirms what we already know: that a business can be established and grown without a detailed plan. It also suggests that many entrepreneurs are more excited by action than planning.

While I'm not going to demand that you create a detailed business plan right now – although there is a time and a place for that – you do need, as a minimum, what I call a Strategy Map and a Long-Range Planner. Each document will fill only a single page and all components within both documents have number restrictions, which forces you to be concise about what's most important. By completing both of these, you will end up with a beautifully simple plan and messaging that's easy to remember and communicate.

The Strategy Map

Your Strategy Map tells anyone involved in your business why you exist and how you are moving towards your goals in the present year. All on a single page. You must communicate your Strategy Map to all of your employees – put it on the office walls so that everyone sees it.

In the sections below, I break down each component of the Strategy Map for you with guidance on how to complete it. I've included examples of large well-known companies for context, along with smaller businesses who we have helped to formulate their strategy – these are marked with an asterisk.

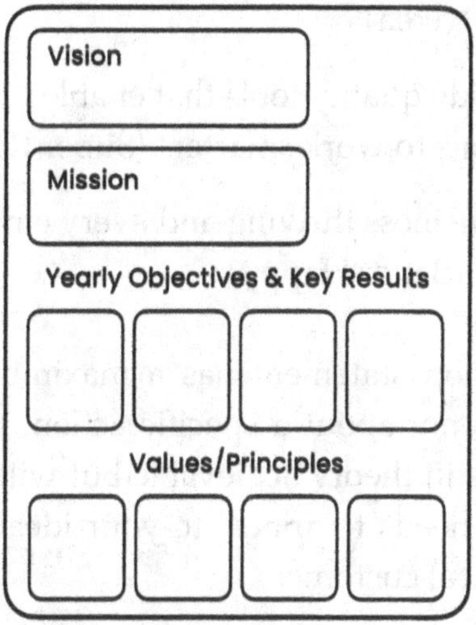

Vision statement

This is a statement about what your business ultimately exists to achieve. It's the goal that you may never reach but that is the motivating force behind everything you do. Although your plans of action might change, your vision should remain broadly similar for the lifetime of your business. A clear vision does two things extremely well:

1. It attracts your ideal customers and employees
2. It enables employees to make independent decisions

Examples:

> 'A world without poverty.'[12] (Oxfam)
>
> 'To create a better everyday life for the many people.'[13] (Ikea)
>
> 'To provide quality tools that enable electricians to work smarter.' (Super Rod)
>
> 'Every business thriving and every employee happy.'[14] (Better Happy)

A good vision statement has a maximum of thirty words. It is not about a specific action. It is an outcome that is in theory achievable but will be difficult to do so. It needs to appeal to your ideal employees and your ideal customers.

Your vision doesn't have to be morally lofty. Take Amazon's original vision statement: 'To be Earth's most customer-centric company; where to build a place people can come to find and discover anything they might want to buy online.[15] They didn't pretend to be someone they weren't to make their vision sound more morally worthwhile. They just got clear on what they actually wanted to achieve.

Some questions to help you get started with crafting your vision statement:

- Why do you do what you do?
- Are you trying to solve a problem? If so, what is it?
- Are you trying to become the best at something? If so, what is it?
- If you achieved everything you wanted to achieve, what change would you see in the world?

Mission

Whereas your vision communicates what you want to achieve, the mission component communicates your unique way of achieving it. You may have a similar vision to other companies but it's unlikely that you'll have both a similar vision and a similar mission. It is essential that you, as the owner, are clear on what makes you different and why your ideal customers and employees will choose you over competitors.

Examples:

> 'Serve consumers through online and physical stores and focus on *selection, price* and *convenience.*' (Amazon)
>
> 'Offer a wide range of *well-designed, functional* home furnishing products at *prices so low* that as many people as possible will be able to afford them.' (Ikea)
>
> 'Facilitate the *transition from dependence to independence* by providing the *highest levels of care,* implementing *effective and innovative solutions.*'[16] (ChangesUK)
>
> 'Provide a range of services and resources that enable optimal levels of *health, happiness* and *business growth.*' (Better Happy)

Each mission statement is a combination of three specific things (in italics) the business is committed to doing well. There are lots of businesses that focus on employee wellbeing, but Better Happy's ideal clients choose us because we focus on health, happiness and business growth.

Questions to help you get started:

- What things are you known for doing particularly well?

- Why do clients choose you over your competitors?
- What do you pride yourselves on doing better than others?

Values/principles

Your values or principles tell you and your team the behaviours and attitudes that your business is based on and are acceptable on your journey to a successful and happy business. From my experience, I have found that it's most effective when companies have a list of the top three to five 'behaviours and attitudes' they want their people to live by.

In the British Army, we had six core values, which is one more than we recommend, but they were easy to remember through the acronym CDRILS: courage, discipline, respect for others, integrity, loyalty, selfless commitment. These core values were drilled into us from day one, and I still remember them more than fifteen years later. These values acted as an unseen guide whenever I had to make decisions.

Many people regard company values as nothing more than a poster on a wall; something to make you look good but never acted on. Genuine values are embodied by you and will help you not only attract the right people, but develop an engaging culture.

Examples:

> 'Customer obsession, passion for invention, commitment to operational excellence and long-term thinking.'[17] (Amazon)
>
> 'Togetherness, caring for people and planet, cost-conscious, simplicity, renew and improve, different with a meaning, give and take responsibility, lead by example.'[18] (Ikea)
>
> 'Be brave, have fun, make a dent.'[19] (Dent Global)
>
> 'Healthy, happy, determined.' (Better Happy)

Notice how again Amazon doesn't pretend to be something they're not. Their values are all focused on growth through customer obsession, not generic buzzwords. Values don't have to be moralistic but they do have to be authentic to you and your company. Also note how Ikea has eight values. This starts to feel like a list instead of something you can easily relate to and remember.

Questions to get you started:

- What employees have you got/had that you would love to clone and why?
- What employees would you never want again and why?

The Long-Range Planner

The Long-Range Planner (LRP) guides you to create long-term plans that ensure your vision is aligned to your goals. The LRP works backwards from ten years in the future to one, because all good strategies start with the end in mind. It is not a highly detailed business plan so it fits onto a single page. Of course, it is impossible to accurately predict what will happen in ten years' time, but that doesn't mean you shouldn't plan ahead. After all, if you don't ask, you don't get.

I recommend you complete this full document with your leadership team, if you have one, as a yearly exercise. Allow a full working day for the first time you do it. We will discuss what planning/meetings you should have and how much time to allocate to them in the performance chapter.

Ten-year success

Unlike your vision, which should be virtually impossible to achieve, your ten-year success *is* possible but should be a stretch. You don't need to go into too much detail here. Choose two to four metrics that, in your eyes, would show that your company is successful ten years from now. Below are a simple and complex example of a ten-year success metric.

- Simple: £20 million in revenue, 15% profit.
- Complex: £50 million in revenue, 10% profit, fifty employees and ten locations across the UK.

Don't let your current confidence levels or belief system hold you back. Ask yourself: if everything goes *perfectly,* what would we like to achieve?

Three-year plan

Your three-year plans are closer to your current reality, so your predictions can become more detailed and accurate. Include your revenue and profit target along with five to ten other success measures.

These measures often include: sources of income, innovation goals, size of team, number of locations, marketing targets, reputation/awards, etc.

One-year objectives

The closer to the present day, the more time you need to spend on planning. Your one-year objectives are pivotal in creating an engaging environment of efficiency and innovation instead of a stressful environment of busyness.

For yearly and quarterly planning, I recommend you use a process called objectives and key results (OKRs). We will go deeper into the psychology of OKRs and how they support growth without burnout in the performance chapter, but for now you just need to know the basic principles:

- You can have no more than five overall objectives for the year – start with three and only add more if essential.
- The objectives should be motivational statements but not specific.
- Each objective needs one to five key results that show it has been achieved.
- Where possible, involve your leadership team in the setting of OKRs.

Some OKR examples:

> **Objective**: Have a record year in sales.
>
> **Key results**: £15m turnover, £5m from new clients, 10% profit.
>
> **Objective**: Be a great place to work.
>
> **Key results**: Employee happiness scores in top 20%, get a Better Happy Workplace award, employee turnover reduced from 20% to 15%.
>
> **Objective**: Supercharge our innovation.
>
> **Key results**: Release ten new products, one breakthrough product sells over £2m, win an industry innovation award.

You can see how, without the key results, the objective is inspiring but 'woolly'. Most people and teams resist applying key results because of the fear of failure that comes with them. If you want to create a happy and inspiring place to work, you have to create an environment where it's better to aim big and fall a little short than it is to set boring goals and achieve them 100%. It's better to achieve 70% of 100 than it is to achieve 100% of 50.

When looking at your final set of OKRs, ask yourself and the team the question: 'If we had only achieved these objectives this year, would we have had a great year?' If the answer is yes, you've done a good job.

Although all this planning might feel like a lot of work, it's a liberating process, as the below story shows. You can access the Long Range Planner and OKR templates at www.betterhappybusinessclub.com/book-bonus.

STRATEGY DEEP DIVE: Alan's story

Alan is the owner of a care company. He had run the business for eight years and had lost the love for it. Like a typical entrepreneur, he created the business for freedom but now felt it was a ball and chain. He stopped going into work as much and the leadership team felt stressed as they had no clear direction when Alan wasn't present. The business was turning into a lose/lose.

I told Alan and the team that we needed to take what was in Alan's head and turn it into an actionable road map. We got the team together and went to work on communicating the vision and mission. Unsurprisingly, they were more aligned than they realised and the vision and mission came together relatively quickly. The difficulty came as we got into the LRP and yearly objectives. There were differing opinions on where the business should be heading and what should be prioritised. Working through this process brought the team closer together and after two full days they had agreed upon a Strategy Map and plan.

The next day, the operations director called me. He wanted to thank me for the work we had done. The clarity they'd gained had given everyone a sense of direction. But what he wanted to thank me for most was helping to reignite Alan's spirit. He explained that everyone knew that Alan wasn't himself, and hadn't been for a few years, but going through this process had opened Alan's eyes to the fact that the business should thrive without him having to be there every day.

Summary

Having a clear and simple strategy in place will improve both the performance of your business and the lives of your employees. Where most businesses try to do everything at once and are in a constant state of stress, yours will morph into an efficient machine. Everybody in your business will know exactly what you want to achieve, what to prioritise and what to say no to.

The businesses that will thrive in the future are the ones who are disciplined in doing less and doing it better – yours is now one of them. You and your employees will know exactly who you are, what makes your business unique and why your customers choose you. This self-awareness will present itself as pride and clarity throughout your teams and in a great customer experience.

Finally, your leadership team and employees will be empowered to make strategic decisions that help grow the business. You, as the business owner, will have a sense of freedom. With the right team in place, you now have confidence that your business could not only function but grow without you.

You've created the roadmap for growth. Now you need to ensure the work environment is one that keeps people engaged and motivated so that they can follow it.

FOUR
Engagement

Through your work in the last chapter you created a clear picture of what long-term success looks like for your business and a map of the milestones you need to reach along the way. Now you need to not only attract the right people to help you achieve those goals but also create an engaging environment in which they can thrive.

By following the simple steps in this chapter, you will make your business engaging and so will stand out to both customers and employers as different. The feelings among you and your team will shift from stress and worry to excitement and fun. Stay consistent in making engagement a priority and soon the people aspect of your business will take care of itself, with or without your presence.

If you choose not to prioritise engagement, you risk your business journey feeling like an uphill battle. The people aspect, which should be one of the most rewarding parts of business ownership, will have an undertone of constant stress and instability. Although lots of businesses talk about engagement, the reality is that the majority of the business world doesn't fully understand employee engagement and isn't making it a priority (as we'll learn later in the chapter). That means it's a golden opportunity for you to get ahead and position yourself as a leader in this area. The business with the best people and best culture wins.

What is engagement?

Engagement carries slightly different meanings in different contexts. It can be used to describe:

- How many people pay attention to a piece of content we put out
- How much we enjoy a film and get into the story
- Two people making an agreement to marriage
- A commitment to a time or date
- Being preoccupied with an activity/person and 'closed off' to others

The common theme across the different uses of the word is some form of relationship. It will be useful for you as a business owner or leader to think of engagement in levels. When there is a relationship between a person and a thing, there is engagement. The higher the level of commitment to that relationship, the higher the level of engagement. This doesn't always directly correlate to the length of the relationship. For example, a person might watch a thirty-second video or view a Van Gogh original and be deeply engrossed in that experience. Although they are only in that relationship for a short period, there is a high level of engagement during that time. The outcome is that the person is left wanting more of that experience and will seek out further work from the creator.

By creating an engaging environment in your workplace, you will create high levels of employee motivation. These are employees who are not just there to do the minimum required of them in order to get paid, but employees who genuinely care about – and so are genuinely committed to – your business and its growth. The bad news is that data suggests that our overall levels of employee engagement in the UK are abysmal. In their 2023 State of the Global Workplace Report, Gallup says that the UK has overall engagement levels of 10%.[20] This places us thirty-third of the thirty-eight countries in Europe, five from bottom. The good news is that this makes it easy for you to get ahead and stand out.

Why now?

It is difficult to sift through all of the potentially good ideas and prioritise which to focus on now. A good leader will have a lot of projects sitting in the 'right thing, wrong time' bucket. But engagement should be one of your top priorities right now. That's because it's good for business. It also makes your business *enjoyable* – for you and your people. There are lots of things you can do to increase sales/profits but not as many that do this while simultaneously making things more enjoyable. Prioritising engagement is one of them.

More data shows that businesses with employee engagement levels in the top 21% grow their profits three times faster than similar competitors with low levels of engagement.[21] It makes sense that businesses with engaged employees make more money, have happier customers, experience less absence and make fewer mistakes. So if it's such a no-brainer, why are most businesses neglecting it?

For two very important reasons:

1. In the past, when the foundational business systems were created – the systems that most businesses are based on today – employee engagement was not important.
2. The mind of the employee and the needs of your business have changed, creating

a perfect alignment opportunity that isn't being recognised.

Understanding these will give you a competitive edge, so let's dig deeper. First, the widely accepted foundational columns of a successful business are sales, marketing, product/service delivery and development, admin, and finance. Although people have always been important for growing a business, engaging them hasn't. For much of modern history in the UK there has been mass unemployment and high levels of poverty. In that kind of economic environment, people are desperate for money, so businesses had an endless supply of people willing to work hard and only had to offer the minimum acceptable wages. In summary, the simple reason most businesses today aren't prioritising employee engagement regardless of its proven benefits is because the crowd isn't doing it, and the crowd isn't doing it because in the past it wasn't important.

Second, is the opportunity of perfect alignment between the needs of your business and the minds of your employees. One of the most satisfying aspects of my job is sharing this simple insight with leadership teams because it always creates the 'Aha' moment – the realisation of how much better their businesses can be. When sharing this idea, I see leaders shift from viewing employee engagement as a challenge to an exciting opportunity. To make it easy to follow, below is a basic model of Abraham Maslow's widely cited and appreciated Hierarchy of Needs.[22, 23]

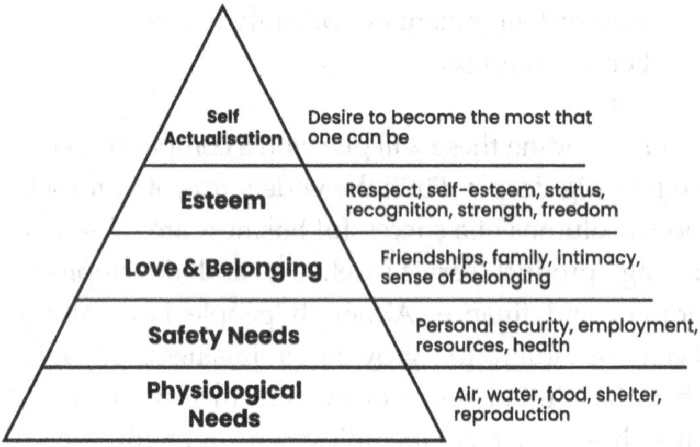

As humans, we are all different but also share a lot in common. Maslow's Hierarchy of Needs shows how humans naturally progress through a series of psychological needs. As one need is fulfilled, we tend to then focus on fulfilling the next. For most of human history, up until very recently in the UK, a person's life has predominantly been consumed with seeking to attain the first two levels of the pyramid: avoiding poverty and trying to ensure survival. During this time, all that employees wanted from work was the thing that supported their survival: pay.

This started to change post World War Two but has more rapidly shifted since the turn of the twenty-first century. Although there are still challenges and struggles, today the average person in the UK has an extremely comfortable life and doesn't worry about true poverty. Even if a person can't find work, they are still virtually guaranteed a standard of living our recent ancestors couldn't dream of.

This means that, for the first time in human history, an increasing proportion of employees are looking for something else, something more from their work. Pay is still important but it's no longer the primary motivator. Belongingness (meaningful relationships), self-esteem (personal and confidence development) and self-actualisation (becoming the best version of oneself) are now creeping up the priority list. Simply paying people a wage without also providing these things might enable you to hold onto employees but they won't be highly motivated, and they will be easily tempted by other employment opportunities.

In the same time period, technology has dramatically altered the way in which businesses operate – and will continue to do so at an exponential rate. Businesses in any industry have to become more agile. For a business to be agile, it needs engaged employees. The non-engaged employee does the minimum that is required of them and will do their best to avoid anything new or out of routine because it requires effort. Trying to not only keep up with but thrive in today's rapid pace of change is a miserable task if you have disengaged employees, but an enjoyable one if your teams are engaged.

The new demands of businesses are perfectly aligned to the new psychological needs of employees. The modern employee doesn't want a transactional relationship where they trade time for money. They want more from their work and are willing to give more in return. Focus on giving your employees what they need, and they'll do the same for your business.

Engagement systems

You might think that all this makes sense and that you, as a good leader, can intuitively create an engaging environment. I'm here to tell you that you can't – you need systems. This is for two reasons. The first is that, regardless of your good intentions, you probably won't do what you think you will. The second is that you can't – and shouldn't – always be in the business.

We like to think we're naturally going to create a great culture, but the reality is that we don't. Business owners and leaders are self-motivated and goal-driven. You're willing to delay gratification in the pursuit of a better future. Most employees are the opposite of that – that's why they're employees not business owners themselves.

Without systems in place, this can cause friction between owners and teams, which decreases engagement levels across the board. You constantly come up with good ideas and enthusiastically take them to the team assuming they will be just as motivated as you are to see them in action. The team are not only overwhelmed by the constant stream of new ideas but often demotivated because this pulls them away from finishing and refining existing projects. Owners can perceive this as negativity or a lack of motivation, and a vicious circle is created.

Nobody wakes up in the morning and thinks, 'I can't wait to go to work today, disagree with my boss and do the minimum that is required of me.' The reason engagement levels are so poor in the UK isn't because people aren't motivated but because the systems in place aren't designed to bring out the best in people, simply because that's never been important before. Let's change this in your business.

Measuring engagement

If you want to improve something, you have to measure it. The only way to accurately measure employee engagement is through anonymous surveys. Of all the systems I recommend, this is the one that owners and leaders resist the most. They are afraid of the results they might get and what that could lead others to think of them. Park those worries to the side and start doing it.

There are countless providers of software that measures employee engagement for you. Each has a unique approach with its own pros and cons. At Better Happy, we prefer to use a company called Friday Pulse, for three reasons:

1. They provide you with real-time data, sending your employees a quick weekly pulse survey year-round.
2. Each quarter, a deeper dive survey is done that provides you and your leadership team with valuable insights into what's going on.
3. Friday Pulse measures 'employee happiness', which is perfectly aligned to our focus at Better Happy.

You can use whichever provider you like, what's important is that you start collecting this data – and then communicate and act on it. Sending out surveys and following up with radio silence sends the wrong message to your employees. It implies you're doing the surveys because they make the company look good, not because you care. You can address this by making employee engagement/employee happiness one of your yearly objectives and work the data into your quarterly planning cycle (covered in the performance chapter).

Permission to have fun

The third level on Maslow's Hierarchy of Needs shows us that people want belonging. Meaningful relationships are one of the most powerful things your business can offer to current and future employees. The problem is that, in an increasingly digital fast-paced world, the power of relationships is neglected in the workplace. This is further hampered by remote and hybrid working, which are both fantastic but also bring new challenges.

Without a system, the reality is you and your people will not spend quality time together. You will spend all your time just being busy. To address this, we created the Proactivity Planner. This dictates minimum viable meeting requirements for managers and leaders. Some of the important events this planner covers are:

- Days with your team
- Personal development planning sessions
- Team socials
- Team health challenges
- Weekly team meetings

We will go through this tool in detail in the next chapter. For now, accept that you will have to proactively plan for people throughout your business to spend structured time together. If you don't, people fall into silo working and loneliness ensues.

Power profiling

The fourth level of Maslow's Hierarchy of Needs tells us that people crave self-esteem. Ultimately, everything covered in this book will help improve the confidence of everyone in your business, but a powerful way to help people from day one is by profiling them.

Profiling tools give people insights into personal preferences, strengths and traits that they often aren't consciously aware of. When you profile someone and help them to interpret and understand the results, you do two things: you help develop their level of self-awareness, and you develop your own level of understanding about that person. Profiling people sends the message that you are genuinely interested in them and that they are important to you.

Make it a standard operating procedure that everyone in your business is profiled. Working this into the first two weeks of onboarding is a simple way to guarantee this happens. It doesn't need to be expensive or time consuming; there are free versions of most good profiling tools available online today. We have found that working through a selection of profiling tools with people and then summarising the results on a single page works best. We've created a template for this called the Power Profile.

To ensure profiling leads to engagement benefits and doesn't feel like a tick-box exercise, make sure that:

- Everyone's profiles are easily visible
- Team members talk other team members through their results
- Profiles are referred to and considered in team meetings
- Profiles are referred to in personal development sessions

Three of our favourite profiling tools are Strengths, DiSC and KOLBE. Other popular profiles include Myers Briggs, Insights and Enneagram. If you prefer to keep things simple, pick one you like and use it with everyone. The process is more important than the actual results.

Personal Development Process

If you want your employees to genuinely care about the success of your company, you have to show them that you genuinely care about *their* success. The highest level of Maslow's Hierarchy of Needs tells us that people crave 'self-actualisation', defined as reaching one's highest potential. Show your employees that their success is important to you, and you'll unlock levels of loyalty and motivation most businesses can only dream of.

To make this easy, I'm giving you a tried and tested process as well as a template that works: the Better Happy Personal Development Process (PDP). The number one reason people don't do this is because of the time it takes. I promise you that the time you invest into this process will pay for itself ten times over. You'll learn things about your people and business you previously had no idea about. You will also kill that dreaded problem of the seemingly happy team member dropping an unexpected resignation on your desk. People will of course, still leave, but rarely will it be unexpected.

All employees should be taken through a PDP with their line manager quarterly (though make sure that no one is responsible for more than eight people). Initially, you will deliver these to your leadership team. The PDP process should take between 40–90 minutes; it's normally longer the first time but quicker thereafter.

I have provided a template for the PDP in the free tools link but I'll give you an overview of the format here. The standard appraisal process consists of a set of questions on how the person thinks they have performed at work. You can access this here: www.betterhappybusinessclub.com/book-bonus.

The Better Happy PDP covers three sections that shift the emphasis from the feel of a 'performance review' to a 'how can I help you' conversation. The first section is a discussion about the person and how satisfied they are in different areas of their life. The second section is the standard performance review with a check against KPIs – if you have them in place. In the third section, together the line manager and employee create a set of personal and professional objectives.

This process makes it easy for you and your managers to play the role of a coach. It radically alters the cultural experience employees have from 'please do your job and if you don't, we'll address it by spending time with you' to 'you, your performance and your goals are important to us and we're here to help you reach your highest potential.' If you and your leadership team are nervous about doing these, a simple but effective hack is to tell the person that you haven't done this before and you're learning as much as them.

ENGAGEMENT DEEP DIVE: Becca's story

Becca is the manager of a customer service department in a hospitality business. It's a demanding job and the team had seen high levels of employee turnover. The employees that remained weren't happy either. 'It's a reactive role and our job is pretty much to respond to complaints,' Becca told me. 'I know the team isn't overly happy but I'm not sure if there's anything I can do about it; it's just a hard job.'

I recommended that Becca take the time to profile the team and take them through the PDP process. Previously, they would do a yearly appraisal (if they stuck around for a year, that is) that covered performance only. Becca emailed me a few weeks later with the results.

'Doing these things has been a massive win. I profiled the team and we went through the results together. I couldn't believe how much they loved learning more about themselves and each other. It was also eye opening for me to see the different profiles and how they all come together. The biggest thing, though, has been the PDP process. The appraisal process felt like a drain for everyone but this has been great. My team has been opening up to me. I've learned loads about them and their goals. They had so many incredible ideas between them and, because I know their goals now, I know if they're planning on leaving or staying. It's not going to make the job better or completely fix employee turnover but it's strengthened my bond with the team and given me a clearer picture of what's going on. Before, I worried daily about who might be handing their notice in, whereas now I've got a pretty clear picture of who's coming, who's going and what we need to do to keep people motivated.'

Summary

Driving high levels of employee engagement in your business will be transformational, not only in how you and your team experience your business but in how it performs. This chapter provides proven systems to improve engagement in a way that stays consistent as the business grows. Embedding these systems and processes will remove the need for you as the owner/leader to keep engagement up through your presence and personality, taking the weight from your shoulders.

Returning to our journey analogy, by getting clear on your strategy you plotted the inspiring destination on the map. This was the first pillar for making your business a happy place to work. Through the work you've done in this chapter, you've created an engaging team environment that will keep your team motivated and committed to the business. Now we need to make sure that the journey is enjoyable and that we don't let workplace politics or our high levels of motivation work against us. When people are passionate, they can easily fall out or work so hard they burn out. In the next two chapters, we'll learn how to make sure that doesn't happen.

FIVE
Leadership

Some 300,000 years ago, *Homo sapiens* (that's us) emerged on earth. We lived the hunter-gatherer lifestyle until we established agriculture, approximately 12,000 years ago. The life of a hunter-gatherer was consumed by one key goal: survival. Survival was difficult and only possible through teamwork. As a result, it's deeply embedded in the human psyche to crave and enjoy working with others towards meaningful goals. But a meaningful goal and a group of people is not enough to create an environment of meaningful teamwork. Humans, like many animal species, require leaders in order to work cooperatively and effectively. Good leadership makes group work effective and enjoyable.

In this chapter, we will get clear on the role leadership plays in your business, why so many businesses struggle with it and, most importantly, how to get it right. Ironically, I've learned that it is purpose-driven leaders who struggle most with leadership, as they can find it difficult to achieve a balance between supporting their people and prioritising their goals. This chapter will show you why this struggle is so common and how to overcome it.

No matter how aligned we are in our passion and commitment towards a goal, without good leadership, group work can become inefficient and downright hostile. To fully utilise the goodwill of your people and to contribute to their happiness and the success of your business, great leadership is required.

What is leadership?

Simply put, leadership is the action of leading a group. From our perspective, anybody in your business who is making strategic decisions – that is, influencing goals in the time frame of one year and over – is in a leadership role. That might be just you or you could have a leadership team. In fact, almost anyone in your business could play a leadership role at some point. By implementing the right behaviours and principles, you create a culture that breeds the behaviours you want to see throughout your business.

Think of leadership as 'leading the ship'. Everyone in your business plays a role moving the ship forwards. The leadership team plots the direction and communicates the plan in a way that inspires and motivates the team to keep up momentum and make progress. We work with lots of business owners who are struggling because they have lost sight of the plan. The movie *The King's Speech* shows King George crippled with a self-doubt-induced stammer, rendering him unable to lead his country during the build-up to World War Two. Through determination he overcomes his challenges and delivers an inspiring speech that boosts the morale of the British people, preparing them for war. Struggling on your journey is not a sign of weakness but a necessary step on the path to achieving truly meaningful goals. Leadership is not about unwavering confidence, that's arrogance. Leadership is about having so much belief in your vision that you can rise from the inevitable periods of self-doubt.

I'm sorry to have to tell you that good leadership won't happen organically. Each of us would like to believe that we will naturally become great leaders. It would also be helpful for us if the people we place into leadership roles – often employees who have come through the ranks – automatically became great leaders too. While this might sometimes happen, it usually doesn't. Without knowledge of and some structure around leadership, it tends to develop in a way that is detrimental to the leader, the team and the business.

This is why in most teams there is more frustration and inefficiency than there is fulfilment and progress.

A clear goal combined with goodwill and wages is not enough to create enjoyable synergy, hence the need for leadership. Humans are emotional beings. These emotions make it virtually impossible for us to work closely as a team without leadership. This is documented well in *The Five Dysfunctions of a Team* by Patrick Lencioni.[24] Lencioni highlights that because humans are emotional, they engage in behaviours that, without leadership, aren't conducive to synergy and growth. For example:

- Self-doubt leads to the avoidance of taking on new challenges.
- Fear of being judged leads to the avoidance of setting clear measures of success.
- Fear of conflict leads to people not being open and honest about how they feel, instead holding onto resentment.

All this means that, without guidance, groups of humans will inevitably become dysfunctional. It's not unusual when I'm working with a team who feel stressed and unhappy with each other that I can point out, 'Have any of you noticed that you all want exactly the same thing?'

The role of a leader is not just to set the direction and inspire the team but to create an environment in which the team can work harmoniously. This is where many leaders, especially business owners, get stumped. Leaders are vision-driven and future-focused. These are great qualities for strong leadership but they can also present as impatience and intolerance. Being a *strong* leader doesn't automatically mean you are going to be a *great* leader.

To be a great leader, you have to embrace the maxim 'What got you here won't get you there.' You have to move away from being aggressively growth-focused and thinking that everyone should be like you, and shift towards creating an inspiring vision-driven environment that brings out the best in people and allows rewarding teamwork. I'm going to show you exactly how to do that.

Personal leadership

There's a new but important dynamic to understand when it comes to leadership. Modern technology has changed the way we live. These changes bring about many new opportunities and challenges. We can work faster and better than ever before, but we also have the possibility of being connected to our work twenty-four-seven. Work has increased exponentially, in both volume and speed. You and the majority of your employees will have the genuine desire to do a great job in your business. You will also suffer from imposter syndrome and perfectionism. Looking at this as an equation makes clear the new problem that businesses face:

> Ability to work any time + Desire to do a
> great job + Lack of self-belief
> = Unhealthy working habits

Various studies suggest that 49% of employees work unpaid overtime and 50% of business owners work from 50–60 plus hours per week.[25] No matter how much you and your people care about your business, when you consistently work too much because of stress, a loss of motivation and, eventually, burnout will follow. An overworked, demotivated team can survive but won't thrive. To make your business a win/win culture in the modern environment you need to not only inspire through team leadership, but prevent unhealthy overworking through personal leadership. Great leaders today need to inspire growth, create environments for harmonious teamwork and model the idea that success at work can be achieved without sacrificing one's health and personal life.

If you and your leadership team have not created a healthy relationship with work for yourselves, no matter how good your team leadership is, your business will always be held back by an undercurrent of stress and overwhelm. If, however, you model a healthy relationship with work, alongside solid team leadership, you'll create a growth environment people love to be part of and that most other businesses will not be able to compete with. One of the hardest lessons business owners and their leadership teams have to learn is how to work less and better.

Personal leadership tools

I learned an important lesson from getting burned out in my first business: we're only at risk of burnout when we are genuinely passionate about what we do. As I worked with more owners, managers and leaders across a wide range of businesses, I further realised that people burn out not because the company is throwing too much at them, but because they genuinely care about doing a good job.

As a result, I started training owners, leaders and managers, showing them how working too much was detrimental to them, their teams and the results they cared so much about. They nodded in approval, then carried on doing it. Worse than that, so did I. Even though I was building a business focused on how to improve results by having a healthy relationship with work. I felt like an imposter. What I recognised was that simply understanding that working too much causes burnout doesn't solve the problem, just like knowing that going to the gym is good for your health isn't enough to actually make it happen.

Your subconscious mind has learned that success is achieved by 'working a lot'. That is after all, what gets most people into leadership positions and what enables business owners to get their businesses off the ground. It's also a behaviour that's ingrained in us by the traditional schooling system, where homework is given to kids as young as five.

What we need are systems that force us to rely less on busyness and more on effectiveness, so that results can be achieved without burnout. Systems that rewire the mind to feel comfortable not being constantly busy. The two systems I'm going to present you with now might seem simple, but they've profoundly changed the lives of hundreds of the people we've coached.

The Proactivity Planner

Imagine sailing around the globe without ever checking a map, a compass or the stars. You might be able to do it, but it's going to be way harder than it needs to be. This is what happens in most businesses, where leadership teams don't allow themselves regular time to plan. This happens because:

1. Business owners, managers and leaders have got to where they are through hard work rather than planning.

2. There is never a shortage of important and urgent tasks in any business, and planning is viewed as an important but non-urgent task.

Even though you and your team know planning makes sense, you probably won't do it and almost certainly won't do it enough. The Proactivity Planner solves this issue for you. It provides you and your team with a minimum viable product strategy structure, telling you how often you should meet and how much time should be committed to each meeting. From working with a wide variety of teams across a range of industries, I know that this is the minimum amount of time you need to commit to meeting in order to be effective. Every year, you and your leadership team should get together and fill out these calendars so that your dates are pre-planned. When dates are scheduled and shared the likelihood of them being forgotten or replaced is vastly reduced. Download your copy via the Better Happy Toolbox here: www.betterhappybusinessclub.com/book-bonus.

Cadence Calendar

The Cadence Calendar is another effective tool to help you and your leadership team thrive. Goal- and work-focused people tend to prioritise their work above everything else in their lives. This clearly has risks. When a hyper focus on work is to the detriment of health, relationships and other important areas of life, this creates a lose/lose situation. To simply suggest 'stop being so focused on work' isn't an effective strategy for preventing this issue. It is better to allow the work-loving person to give their work the attention they want to without the underlying worry that other important areas of their life are being neglected.

The Cadence Calendar is a one-page colour-coded table that should be completed quarterly. We issue these to our clients as A3 whiteboards that can be attached to the fridge or placed somewhere they can be seen daily.

The calendar enables you to commit to two daily, weekly and monthly habits that will contribute to your quality of life, and to different activities you would like to do throughout the year. Doing these with a partner is particularly effective.

Examples of **daily habits**:

- 10,000 steps
- Read thirty pages
- Have an hour phone-free with the kids

Examples of **weekly habits**:

- Date night with partner
- Three gym sessions
- Half-day for planning – no meetings

Examples of **monthly habits**:

- Go somewhere new and fun
- Read a personal development book
- Make new investments

The Cadence Calendar reminds hard-working professionals to prioritise themselves by breaking the process into steps that are easily manageable alongside work. When you stick to your Cadence Calendar commitments, they become habits. Your mind learns that good results at work can be achieved alongside improving your personal life. If you are concerned that you or your leadership team is neglecting themselves, focusing on their job at the expense of their personal life, the Cadence Calendar is a game changer.

Team leadership

To lead teams effectively, you have to:

- Have a clear vision
- Communicate that vision in a way that inspires people
- Nurture an environment that enables people to work harmoniously

That all sounds lovely, but it's not that simple. To achieve these things, you have to engage in something that most people will go to great lengths to avoid: conflict.

Conflict has become particularly difficult recently as political and social ideologies are vilifying it so aggressively. As a result, some people seek to create an environment in which everyone has the right to never be offended. While this might sound great, it is unrealistic. Such attempts succeed only in creating an environment where people are cautious about saying what they think. 'Better to just keep quiet and agree than say something that might upset others.' This attitude is terrible for culture, for growth and, ironically, for the thing it purports to protect – people's mental health. When people do not communicate their frustrations:

- Problems that could easily be addressed persist
- Resentments and judgements build up, leading to high levels of stress
- Relationships break down
- A culture of gossiping develops

I've worked with many leadership teams where it's obvious that the most significant barrier to business growth and fulfilment is a lack of healthy conflict. If there is no conflict between your leadership team and wider teams, or within those teams, that means one of two things:

1. Everybody in the business is in perfect alignment.
2. People don't feel comfortable sharing what they truly think.

I'm yet to meet a team that falls into the first category. Leaning into and actively inviting conflict feels nerve-wracking initially, but then two things start to happen. First, you teach your subconscious mind that conflict isn't as dangerous as it thinks it is, which reduces the stress associated with it. Second, you and your team feel an immense sense of lightness as you release frustrations and emotions, leading to better health and faster progress. If this is something you know you particularly struggle with, don't worry – we'll cover it in more detail in Part Three in the chapter on mental health, and explore some specific tools to help.

LEADERSHIP DEEP DIVE: Craig's story

Craig is the owner of a successful business that designs and sells tools. Craig is in his late fifties and starting to think about life after his business. The business employs around fifty people. He is very much the leader of the business. All the staff know and look up to him. He's got a nice lifestyle and isn't in a major rush to leave the business.

When I met Craig, however, he was concerned about the health of the members of his leadership team. He had made the mistake of working too much in the past and changed his ways after a serious health scare. He could see the same passion-driven behaviours in his leadership team but, no matter what he said to them, it didn't seem to make much difference. I explained to Craig that, from personal experience, this is emotional rather than rational behaviour. I told him, 'The combination of passion, the feeling of responsibility and a dose of imposter syndrome means they're likely to continue working in a way that's unhealthy until they get sick or fed up. You need systems to prevent it.'

Craig instantly bought into the process. He got the leadership team together and they scheduled all the dates recommended in the Proactivity Planner. The team went from meeting ad hoc to a structured weekly and monthly meeting cadence. One of the members of the leadership team told me and the rest of the group that she had been feeling disconnected from the team for a long time. Getting into the flow of these meetings reconnected the whole team and supercharged their collaboration to the benefit of the whole business. Meeting regularly and sharing Cadence Calendars also helped the team to not feel overwhelmed. Previously, they had been guilty of simply reacting to everything the business threw at them. Now, during their meetings they are clearly communicating what the priorities are and are not, meaning they all know when to say yes and when to say no. Most importantly, they all close their laptops on time without worrying.

The VACS model

Although no guidance can replace your intuition, at Better Happy we have created the simple VACS model that can guide you and your leadership team in handling conflict and leading effectively. VACS stands for:

- **Vision and values-driven:** The leadership team must inspire and guide growth towards your vision in alignment with your values. Your vision and values should be used to stress-test your decision making, review performance and assess behaviour. When your vision or values are challenged, you will likely need to engage in healthy conflict.

- **Accountability:** To progress towards your vision and uphold your values, you and your team will have to take risks and make commitments. Regardless of the levels of goodwill among you, your leadership team and the people in your business, humans try to avoid doing new things. This is due to the fear of failure and being judged by others. The only way to overcome this is to hold ourselves and others accountable. To do that, you must become masters of identifying objective success measures for any commitments made. We'll cover how to do this in more detail in the next chapter. For now, know that if you don't create systems to keep people accountable, even yourself, the ball will get dropped and things won't get done.

- **Conflict:** Note that as a leader, you have to create an environment where conflict is seen as a necessary part of teamwork. Conflict should be healthy. People need to feel that they can express their emotions and feelings without being directly or indirectly punished. For you and your leadership team, that means you have to get comfortable taking and processing criticism in a productive manner. Whenever your vision or values are being compromised, conflict is required. Whenever accountability is lacking, conflict is required.
- **Supreme team:** Leaders in a business will usually belong to two teams. The team they head up and the leadership team that they are a part of. The natural tendency is to prioritise the team they are leading. This is bad for business. It's essential that the needs of the leadership team are given the highest priority. So many of the issues that plague businesses stem from leaders prioritising their own careers and teams over the needs of the senior leadership team, which represents the business. Your senior leadership team should meet regularly, have clear shared objectives and be held accountable for the commitments made.

You will be able to identify almost any problem you have with leadership or culture by honestly grading yourself and your team out of 10 on the four components of the VACS model. When you're scoring an average of seven or more out of ten on each of the components, you'll be well on your way to a great workplace culture.

Summary

Without the right leadership, a business that should be enjoyable and rewarding becomes stressful. Human emotions get in the way of effective working and people end up getting frustrated with each other even when they share the same goal. But getting your leadership right brings the best out in people, enabling them to enjoy working together towards a common goal. A business with great leadership isn't bogged down by stress and people issues or chronic unhealthy working habits. Disagreements and conflict are easily navigated and recognised as essential parts of the journey. Teams feel great because they're achieving fantastic results while enjoying good health and a thriving personal life. All of this can be a reality in your business, regardless of size or industry. In this chapter, I've given you proven tools that can make this happen. When you apply these tools with a genuine desire to make your business a win/win for everyone, they are extremely powerful.

As you and your leadership team are now committed to healthy working, it's no longer an option to constantly try to do everything yourselves. To shift from a 'busyness' to an efficient business you need processes that enable you to do less, better. You need a system to identify and prioritise what's most important *now*. That's exactly what we're going to put in place in the next chapter.

SIX

Performance

Creating a high-performance environment is crucial to the health of your business and the happiness of you and your people. As we have learned, people are happy when working cooperatively with others towards goals they care about. Everything you have implemented so far has enabled you to create an inspiring environment in which people feel valued and have a genuine desire to do great work. This is the foundation for high performance. But there is one more piece to the jigsaw if you want to make your business a win/win. You now have to put a structure in place that will allow your people to sustainably work towards realising the business's vision, without it becoming a negative force.

The sprinter displays high performance over a short distance but if they try to sustain that pace for 800m, they're going to suffer some serious pain. This is one of the risk factors of combining an inspiring strategy with highly motivated people. They can be so passionate about the goal and pumped up to reach it that they go about it in a way that is unsustainable and that makes them miserable.

I learned this lesson through my own mistakes in my first business and have since realised just how common this problem is. We know that 50% of managers are burned out[26] and over 50% of small business owners suffer with poor mental health.[27] How enjoyable is your work going to be if your manager or business owner is overwhelmed and stressed? Not very.

When you don't have a system to break your long-term goals down into actionable, manageable steps, what was once inspiring becomes a weight around your neck and around the necks of those who want to help. In this chapter I'm going to show you how to create an environment where the ongoing pursuit of your long-term business goals is a positive and rewarding experience for everyone involved. You'll discover the common reasons why the energy can so often become negative and how to side-step this. By the end of this chapter, you'll not only know how to drive consistent growth and prevent burnout, but you'll also have the systems in place so that this growth happens without you. Shifting from an environment where growth is dependent on your presence and ideas to one where it happens organically might just be the most important step in making your business a win/win for all of the Core Four (owner, team, customers, business).

What is performance?

As a business owner and leader of people, your understanding of what performance is can make or break your culture and, ultimately, the level of success you achieve. Get it right and everyone wins, get it wrong and everything in your business feels like hard work.

Performance, in the business sense, is defined in the Cambridge Dictionary as 'how well a person, machine, etc. does a piece of work or an activity.'[28] But to judge how 'well' a person does a piece of work, you have to be clear on the desired results. Knowing what your desired results are is, therefore, essential to measuring performance.

Let's look at some examples:

1. A car could be classed as high-performance if the desired result is a fast 0–60mph acceleration time, but low-performance if the desired result is fuel efficiency.

2. A marathon runner displays high performance in the world of endurance running, but low performance in sprinting.

Without the context of '0–60' or 'fuel efficiency' you leave judgements on performance up to interpretation, and in business that's not good. When businesses aren't clear about desired results, 'effort' or 'hours worked' become the unofficial benchmarks of performance. This is bad for business and bad for people. Busyness becomes the name of the game and whoever stays latest at the office is regarded as the best performer. The worst people for doing this are business owners and highly motivated people who get promoted to management and leadership positions. If you let this run its natural course, you will end up in the same camp as most other businesses – one where your leaders and managers are exhausted, and your team disengaged.

You don't want this as the unofficial performance strategy in your business. The poor results of that are all around us. You want a strategy that creates a win/win, so introduce this simple but profoundly impactful mantra to define your performance strategy:

'Results without burnout'

This statement might seem simple, but it's a paradigm shifter. 'Results without burnout' is the polar opposite to 'who can work the most.' To live by this mantra, you have to create an environment where goals are a priority but don't overwhelm people.

The three zones

After getting burned out in my first business, I knew getting a job wouldn't fulfil me but I also didn't want to go back into business and make myself miserable. I realised that my only option was to figure out how to actually enjoy owning a business. When I looked back over my past mistakes, it became obvious that I had been in a vicious cycle moving from inspired big-picture goal-setting to stress, overwhelm and apathy. The more times I went through this loop, the more my confidence dropped. I knew that to enjoy business – and life in general – I had to find a way to break this cycle. This led to my discovery of the three zones.

Being conscious of these zones has been pivotal in enabling me to have a healthy relationship with the work I love. When I share this concept with people, teams and businesses there's always a big 'Aha' followed by huge changes in behaviour for the better. If you're like the majority, you will be stuck in a cycle moving between Zones 1 and 2. By the end of this chapter, you will have everything you need to move your people and business into Zone 3.

- Zone 1: Comfortably Uncomfortable
- Zone 2: The Passion Problem
- Zone 3: Better Happy

Zone 1: Comfortably uncomfortable

Most people end up spending the majority of their time here. The more you cycle between Zones 1 and 2, the more the culture of your business will want to settle here. In this zone, there is an unofficial but widely accepted resistance towards goal-setting and innovative teamwork.

The day-to-day feel of the business is of just doing the basics to keep the ship afloat. All problems are seen as stressful, growth of any sort feels like an effort and collaboration is virtually non-existent. People are consciously unfulfilled but accept it. It's easier to complain about how things are and do nothing than to try and change anything. This can be perceived as laziness or a lack of willingness, but it's actually driven by fear of failure and of making mistakes, all of which is exacerbated by spending some time in Zone 2.

Zone 2: The passion problem

In this zone, vision and goals shine through but there's no structure for packaging them. As there's still a culture of 'busyness is good for business', people aren't given the time they need to achieve goals. The goal-setting process is rushed, with a lack of collaboration. As a result, goals tend not to be specific, are poorly communicated and lack any sort of associated action plan. Instead of motivating people, goals confuse and overwhelm everybody. The worst part is that businesses, teams and people develop the limiting belief that they can't achieve their goals, so why bother trying? At this point, Zone 1 welcomes you back with open arms, offering a sweet shot of relief.

Zone 3: Better happy

The Better Happy zone is one of enjoyable and sustainable growth. Goals are created, specified and communicated in a way that genuinely motivates people. Everyone is involved in influencing goals, creating a feeling that 'we're driving this change' versus 'this is the next "good idea" creating more work for us.' Goal setting and pursuit is a part of the DNA of the business. Everyone has goals, is supported to achieve them and held accountable for their progress. People don't stress about goals or fear making mistakes because when people are struggling there's a culture that asks, 'what support do you need to progress?' not 'why aren't you performing?'

To sustain a high-performance culture where everybody wins, you need to be in Zone 3. Interestingly, the automatic go-to solution when people or teams think they are struggling with performance is better time management. But when you address the problem holistically, time management is a minor issue. To exist comfortably in Zone 3, the leaders and managers in your business need three things:

1. A healthy mindset around time
2. Measurement of what matters
3. Basic time management skills

Time mindset

The speed at which we can communicate and, therefore, work is increasing at an exponential rate. Internet connectivity is faster and mobile devices and computers are more powerful. We've recently witnessed the widespread introduction of easily accessible artificial intelligence systems that can even speed up our thinking.

This creates endless opportunities but also lots of problems, especially in businesses. When people try to do everything, nothing gets done well. When everything is important, nothing is a priority. The only way people and teams can consistently thrive in the fast-paced modern environment in a sustainable way is through prioritisation. But that requires time. How do you make time for prioritising when there's already too much to do?

You first have to accept that there is always more to do than can ever actually be done in a business. A large proportion of business owners, leaders and managers have spent a lot of their working lives in more junior roles where they worked hard and quickly addressed issues. In customer service roles, for example, high performance might be responding to as many customers as you can, as quickly as possible, in the time available. The faster you are, the more recognition you get. Carrying on with this approach to work will lead to burnout and poor performance once people reach manager level and above. This is part of the reason why there are such high levels of burnout amongst managers and small business owners – many have come directly from more operational roles. These people are doing what has worked for them in the past – and why wouldn't they?

In order to create a win/win, sustainably high-performance culture we have to develop the right mindset – in you and your people, but especially in anybody in a management role. Implementing the tools from this chapter and the rest of the book will help, as will the following mantras:

- There's always more work to be done than can be done.
- Problems are a natural part of business and can't all be solved.
- It's not who does the most that wins, but who does the things best that matter.

Once you develop a healthy relationship with time, strategic planning will enable you to identify what matters most so that you can direct your time towards it.

Measuring what matters

Two streams of activity in your business contribute to its performance and overall growth: the things you already do well, and innovation. Having systems to measure both is important for your business and your people, yet most businesses resist this due to fear.

They fear that by measuring these things, they will stress people out. Remember, we humans are hardwired to want to do a good job. People will become unhappy and stressed not because they're worried about numbers, but because they have no idea if they're doing a good job or not. You might say that your people know they're doing a good job because you or your managers tell them that they are. But what if some days you forget? Humans are emotional and unreliable, but numbers aren't.

Measuring what you already do well

The way to measure what you already do well is through Key Performance Indicators (KPIs). Every person in your business should have three top KPIs that they are responsible for and that they can achieve by doing the basics of their job well. These numbers aren't there to push people to new levels but to hold people accountable to the expected standards. Every person should have a numerical target within a certain range. Let's look at some examples of KPIs in different roles:

- **Business owner:** ## new big client relationships, ##% gross profit.
- **Head of manufacturing:** Average job completion ## days, ## number of returns.
- **Customer services:** ## calls answered, ## tickets closed.

If you have nothing like this in place, don't worry. That's common. Get your team together and make this a group exercise. Explain the benefits of every role having its own KPIs. People tend to play down the value they bring to a business, so ask them:

- What positives does your work add to the business?
- What would go wrong or stop working if you stopped coming to work?
- What are your three biggest impact areas?

Then turn these into numbers. You and your people may resist this process at first because numbers bring with them a fear of judgement. Communicate to your people that without numbers there is no measure of performance, leaving 'busyness' to become the unofficial measure. You want to drive a culture that rewards those who can work the greatest, not the latest – establishing KPIs is the first major step in that process.

Measuring innovation

You measure growth in your business through tracking OKRs. When used right, OKRs are good for the business because they drive innovation and growth, and they're good for your people because they love knowing that they're doing a good job. Everyone will have ideas on how things can be done better. Having an objective and measurable process for tracking this gives people the opportunity to share those ideas and see their impact.

The OKR process we covered in Chapter Three is repeated here but with teams or individuals at a quarterly level (monthly in particularly fast-changing businesses). Each quarter, get your teams together to review the previous quarter and the yearly objectives you have set for the company. They should then set between three and five objectives for their team in the following quarter that they believe will make the most progress towards the company's yearly objectives. The benefits this process brings to your business are priceless:

- Access to potentially game-changing ideas from your teams
- Increased levels of collaboration across people and teams
- High levels of engagement

A vital part of the OKR process is applying measurable key results. The same numbers-based fears arise here as with KPIs, but you have to make this non-negotiable. When measures are in place growth becomes unavoidable and eventually an enjoyable part of your business DNA. Essential to this is checking for key results at every weekly meeting. As we covered in the VACS model, people need accountability. The Proactivity Planner we used earlier provides you with a detailed plan for when to have these meetings and how often.

Some final pointers to get this process off to a flying start:

- Key results should be moon shots – difficult to achieve but possible at a stretch.
- Achieving 70% of a key result should be cause for celebration.
- If you achieve 100% of key results, they were too easy.

You want a culture of true innovation and enjoyable growth (Zone 3). Part of that is getting comfortable with failing. If you have a system that punishes 'failures', everyone will resist the new (keeping you in Zone 1). Now you have KPIs and OKRs in place, performance has an official definition in your business and is no longer about who can work the most. The judgement of performance is also no longer based on subjective human emotions but instead on objective numbers.

PERFORMANCE DEEP DIVE: Sarah's story

Sarah is the learning manager in a large business with over 5,000 staff. Sarah learned about the OKR process on a development course I was leading and the process appealed to her immediately. 'I know this is what we need in our team,' she said. 'We have so much going on and so many good ideas, it can feel overwhelming for my team and me. I want to implement it but I'm not sure where to start and I worry it's hard to create measurable key results for the work that we do.'

As the company was so big, Sarah had to treat her department like a small business in itself. We started by going through the strategy model covered in Chapter Three. Once we had a clear vision, mission and values we could get to work on creating OKRs. After some questioning, we identified four key areas of growth that Sarah and her team wanted to prioritise:

- Make our learning great, enjoyable and more accessible
- Make our onboarding process fantastic
- Create a visual career progression map for employees with tailored learning solutions aligned to each role

Sarah and the team were agreed that if they achieved those three objectives on top of their day-to-day, they would have had a year worth celebrating. Next, we worked on key results. I won't list them all here but what I will say is that everything was measurable. I asked the team, 'How do we know that the learning isn't great, enjoyable and accessible already?' The replies included, 'Our training days aren't getting booked up' and, 'Only X amount of managers have completed this training.' These answers led to clear key results such as: 90% booking rate for training days, and 80% of managers trained in X. Sarah told me later that, although she knew the key results would likely change, just having them in place had made a huge difference for her and the team. They've gone from saying yes to everything and trying to do it all, working in a state of flux, to having a clear plan and knowing when to say no.

Time management

Time management gets more attention than it deserves. Much of the stress and overwhelm people face in business will be solved through the previous steps in this chapter. When people have specific measures of success, clear deadlines and objectives that have been broken down into manageable tasks with weekly check-ins, the need for 'time management' decreases significantly. That said, there are some simple principles for better time management that will benefit you and your managers, so let's briefly discuss those:

- **Own your week:** Every Friday or Monday, plan the week ahead to ensure you have time for everything non-reactive: meetings, strategy, objectives, supreme team commitments. If there are too many tasks and too little time, communicate that to your peers instead of trying to manage it all – this will only create a false economy.
- **Own your day:** Every day, be clear on the top three things you must achieve to make that day a success. This will stop you overcommitting yourself and spending your entire day reacting to problems and the needs of others.

The basics of good time management don't need to be any more complicated than this. There are countless theories out there to help you better manage your time but from experience, most of these are sought out as a distraction from deeper issues. When everyone is clear on the goals and what is expected of them, time management becomes simple. If you or your people are still struggling with time when all of these systems are in place, it's likely more of a self-confidence issue – commonly imposter syndrome, leading to perfectionism. In which case, the mental health chapter in Part Three will help.

Summary

Creating an environment of high performance benefits your business and people in many ways. The common view of high performance is that it is high intensity, high pressure and only for the elite. At Better Happy, we view it as results without burnout. By adding the 'without burnout' component we guide businesses not just to prioritise results but to do so in a way that is sustainable. The sustainable approach wins in the long race.

The work people do is a key ingredient of their overall happiness in life. Humans have always craved meaningful work and meaningful relationships, and they can find both in the workplace. Regardless of what industry your business is in, it solves some form of problem and provides both meaningful relationships and work to your people. Just paying people and giving them a job description is not enough to create harmony. In the past it was, and so many of the systems businesses rely on today still lean on outdated principles. Through implementing the first four components of the SELPH model I've presented in Part Two you can create an environment where you, your people and your business win. We've talked about how to bring out the best in people. When you have a business that supports, attracts and retains happy, passionate and motivated people, you can solve any problem and achieve any goal.

PART THREE
STEP FIVE OF SELPH – HEALTH

Most people and businesses are held back by ill health and see it as a challenging obstacle to overcome. Happy businesses see health as an opportunity and effortlessly create cultures that support optimal health amongst their people. Part Three of this book will show you how to be one of these businesses.

Good health isn't essential to good business but it's a no brainer. A win/win. Most of the health issues that plague businesses are actually symptoms of a poor culture, which we have already addressed through the first four steps of the SELPH model. Nevertheless, health problems can still arise in a company with a great culture and a great leader knows how to proactively deal with or prevent these.

When health is neglected or only dealt with reactively, businesses are held back by low productivity and preventable absence. Business owners who don't look after their own health are particularly prone to serious consequences due to the mentally demanding nature of the role.

Creating a top–down culture of good health in your business isn't difficult. Following these simple steps to foster optimum health in your own life and for your people will improve everyone's performance.

In the three chapters of this final part, we will cover:

- How to use your business as a vehicle for better health
- The basics of mental health and how to support mental thriving in yourself and among your people
- The basics of physical health and how to support physical thriving in yourself and among your people

By the end of Part Three, you will no longer see health as a challenge to be overcome in business but as an opportunity to be grasped.

SEVEN
Health

When you started your business, I doubt you ever considered that one day you would feel a level of responsibility for or stress about the health of future employees. There's so much to think about when starting and growing a business that your own health, never mind that of your employees, is understandably way down the priority list. Unfortunately, my experience shows me that, for most business owners, health only becomes a priority once it becomes a problem. You wake up one day and the pain in your back is so severe you can't put your socks on let alone get to work, or one of your best performers goes on long-term sick leave due to stress-related issues. I've worked with two business owners who didn't start prioritising their health until they had early heart attacks. Another went through a terrible cancer diagnosis, which they were convinced their unhealthy relationship with work had contributed to.

I'm not sharing these examples to scare you but to highlight how common it is to neglect health in the pursuit of business goals, and the type of consequences that could eventually lead to. Your health and the health of your people plays a strong role not just in the potential growth of your business but also in making the most of the only thing of real value any of us have: the present moment.

What health means and why it matters

We all know that health is important and that we should probably make more of an effort with it. But if I asked you what good health actually means, could you answer? The Cambridge Dictionary defines health as 'the condition of the body and the degree to which it is free from illness, or the state of being well.'[29]

It's interesting that this definition only considers the physical body. When I owned my first business and didn't handle my stress levels well, I was in good shape physically, but I was miserable and wouldn't have described myself as healthy. The Cambridge Dictionary defines mental health as: 'the condition of someone's mind and whether or not they are suffering from any mental illness.' Taking both these definitions into account, it's fair then to say that overall health is the combination of both physical and mental health.

As business owners, it's important that we create cultures of good health for ourselves and our teams. While poor health might be identified through the presence of illness/disease, *good* health is not merely the absence of illness or disease. You can be 'not sick' but also not particularly well. It's helpful to think of your health status as falling into one of three zones:

- Unhealthy, where one is clearly unwell, physically or mentally
- Neutral, where one is not sick but also not thriving
- Healthy, where one feels good both physically and mentally

The majority of people in wealthy developed countries bounce between the unhealthy and neutral zones. They don't live healthy lives and don't think too much about health because there are no major issues. They don't feel great, but they are able to get through their days, do what's required of them and relax at weekends. Although they are not in the 'unhealthy' zone they are slowly and consistently moving towards it. When, eventually, an issue does arise that places them in the unhealthy zone, they take reactive action to address the issue. A new diet is followed, physio exercises are practised, a meditation or activity regime is undertaken. It's the same pattern that we saw with the three zones in Chapter Six. In most cases, once the issue has resolved or reduced, the person returns to their old pattern of behaviour and begins a slow and consistent journey back to the unhealthy zone.

Why does all of this matter to you as a business owner? Let's be realistic: you can absolutely run a successful business without thinking about or prioritising health. People who say good health is essential for business are talking nonsense. The majority of businesses don't understand and support health among their people and many of them function just fine. But that's not to say that those same businesses aren't bogged down with inefficiencies such as low productivity and high sickness absence, that a small amount of understanding and effort around health could solve. They also don't reach anywhere near their full potential. While good health isn't essential, poor health is definitely bad for business.

Then of course there's you, as the owner. You are doing one of the highest stress jobs out there. If you don't look after your health, at best you'll be off your A-game and at worst you'll put yourself in an early grave. As a wise mentor of mine once said, 'you don't want to be the most successful person in the graveyard.'

Employee health

If you try to support the health of your employees because you think you *have to,* you will go about it reactively and it will feel like an uphill battle. The health of an employee is ultimately the responsibility of the employee, not the employer. Suggesting otherwise risks creating a culture of entitlement where employees relinquish all responsibility for their wellbeing and blame any health issues on their employer. This happens a lot. For clarity, the Health and Safety at Work Act[30] legislates that businesses must control risks to the health and safety of their employees. Controlling risk is very different to taking full overall responsibility for the health of an employee.

You should support the health of your employees (and yourself) because you want to and because it's good for business. Across the board we're not very good at this, for two reasons.

1. Maintaining a baseline of good health used to happen on autopilot

Having to consciously look after your health is a relatively new concept for people in the UK. Less than eighty years ago, most jobs were active in some way or another, food supplies were more limited, processed foods were not widely available and the internet didn't exist. This meant that, without any conscious effort, people had a baseline of good health. They were active and ate smaller amounts of more whole foods (foods that haven't been processed). As people didn't have the internet, they socialised in person and didn't have the means to constantly compare their lives to millions of others'. There were, of course, still many health issues and life expectancy was overall lower, due to a variety of issues such as poor living and working conditions, a poorer economy and a lack of quality healthcare in comparison to today. But these things tended to be unavoidable; things that were the product of circumstance, rather than things you could avoid if you made the effort to.

2. Businesses didn't need employees with good health

Just as they can today, businesses in the past could function even if people weren't healthy. Health just wasn't that important. The ball was in the employer's not the employees' court. Statutory Sick Pay was only introduced in the UK in 1983.[31] Combine this with high levels of unemployment and most jobs consisting of low-skilled, repetitive manual labour and it's clear why health didn't matter. If people aren't well, they don't work, you don't pay them and you quickly replace them with someone else.

Today, the ball is increasingly in the employees' court. Businesses have to become more agile, which can only be achieved with engaged, healthy energised people. A sick person can do simple repetitive tasks but will struggle to work collaboratively with others and utilise innovation to solve problems. If it's hard for them to look after their health and they get to a point where they have issues that prevent them from working, this will have multiple cost implications for your business.

Of course, there are elements of health that are completely outside of our control. No matter how great your workplace or habits, sickness is always a possibility. But much of the sickness that holds teams back is completely preventable – indeed, 22.5% of all deaths in the UK in 2019 were considered avoidable.[32] Your focus should, therefore, be on creating an environment that reduces preventable sickness and helps people thrive. Doing so isn't as difficult as you think.

It's not hard to be healthy

As we've touched on, it's in theory easier for people to be healthy today than ever before. The challenge is that modern life encourages and facilitates poor health. Fortunately, just as your business is perfectly positioned to transform the happiness of employees, it's also perfectly positioned to transform their health. When I owned a group training gym, I quickly realised that it wasn't the workouts or the quality of the coaching that had the biggest impact on the health of our clients. It was the environment. Our clients were busy professionals and business owners who had never been able to make healthy habits stick before. They felt out of place in normal gyms and when they tried things alone, they quickly got bored. When they trained with us, they were in a positive environment around like-minded people. They looked forward to going to the gym and interacting with their community. Because of this they turned up regularly, stayed with us for years and got into great shape. Being healthy became a part of their identity through belonging to the community.

The overall environment and community of the UK is one of disconnect and poor health habits. People spend more time looking at their phones than interacting with others. They don't exercise. Food is rushed and usually processed. We don't like to talk about thoughts and feelings. Instead, we bottle things up and make up for it by spending money, eating, doing drugs or drinking alcohol. Just as we did with the gym, you have the opportunity to create your own subculture in your business. By prioritising health, implementing some super simple systems and modelling healthy behaviours through your leadership team, your business can become something that transforms the health of its employees. If you're willing to make health a priority and put in small amounts of effort, you can achieve this in any business, in any industry.

Perhaps you struggle with health yourself and, although reading this makes you excited at what can be achieved, you quickly feel deflated as the imposter syndrome kicks in. You may ask yourself, 'How can you support health in your business if you struggle to do it for yourself?' and 'Don't you need to be in great shape, physically and mentally, to achieve this?'

Good health is not having a six pack, winning the Tour de France, running a marathon, sitting in meditation for an hour, having an ice bath every morning or climbing Mount Everest. You just need to create a culture where prioritising health is normalised and where the general direction of travel is towards good not poor health. Most people and businesses overcomplicate it and get poor results because they don't want to do the basic, boring stuff.

HEALTH DEEP DIVE: Mark's story

I had just started a health workshop with a group of senior leaders of a large company. This was my third workshop with this particular group and there had been a six-week gap between this session and the last. On the previous training day we had covered nutrition, so I asked the group if anyone had made any positive changes. Mark stuck his hand in the air to share his:

'I took on board what you said about not skipping breakfast every day and my team noticed my actions. I now take a breakfast that includes protein and fruit and eat it at work. Some of the team were interested in what I was eating and why, so I shared with them the basics we had learned. Lots of my team are now eating healthy breakfasts, which really surprised me and, because I'm not starving at lunch, I've lost 8lbs.'

One of the reasons it's easy to be unhealthy is that people are part of the environment and culture that normalises poor health. You and your leadership team can change this. You don't have to become health gurus or fitness fanatics to create an incredible culture of health, you just need to create your own subculture that normalises utilising the modern environment to be healthy, not unhealthy. Most business owners and leadership teams are awful at looking after their health, so that's the culture they unintentionally create. It doesn't matter what you say; it matters what you *do*. Remember – being healthy isn't hard, and in the following chapters I'll show you exactly how easy it can be. Let's look at two simple but transformative tools to make health a part of your culture.

The Why Template

Improving health, like improving any aspect of your life, boils down to effort. When there isn't a compelling reason combined with ample self-belief in the pursuit of a goal, efforts quickly dissipate. Most people struggle to make any progress with their health due to a lack in these two areas. People genuinely want to be healthier but they aren't clear on what that looks like or why it's important to them. They don't know what to do and lack confidence in their ability to make a change. By normalising health in the culture of your business, you will help people to overcome many of these issues because improving health becomes a normal part of the day-to-day routine.

The Why Template is something that line managers can take their direct reports through during their

PDPs. This is especially impactful when people score low for health on the downloadable Wheel of Life chart from the first part of the PDP (covered in Chapter Four).

Through five simple questions, the Why Template helps a person get clear on how health impacts the areas of their life that are most important to them, the impacts of neglecting it and what 'good' looks like for them. This is powerful because lots of people aren't interested in health for the sake of health, but when it's linked to what is important to them they find the drive to make it a priority. This simple to follow template also helps your managers play the role of a coach, which leads to higher levels of employee retention and engagement.

Here are the questions:

- What areas of life are most important to you?
- How does your health impact these areas?
- What will the impact of maintaining or improving your health be on these areas?
- What will the impact of neglecting your health be on these areas?
- Considering this, what does good health look like for you? Be specific.

You can download the template at www.betterhappy-businessclub.com / book-bonus.

Community challenges

Done right, challenges are a fantastic way to make health a part of your culture and have a big impact on everyone's lives and on your business. Challenges also enable you to involve everyone in the company without having to take people out of the business. As you will see over the next two chapters, you can broadly define health into four categories of movement, nutrition, sleep and mind. This works well for challenge planning as you can cover all of these areas through one four-week challenge per quarter. Remember that transforming people's health isn't about fixing all of their issues with one all-encompassing solution but about normalising prioritising and making an effort with health so that people are constantly moving in the right direction. Challenges are a perfect way to do that.

The key to good challenges is simplicity and buy-in. We have found that the best ways to achieve this are through:

- **Teams and team leaders:** Breaking the business up into teams or departments and allotting a team leader for each. This should be a positive people person who likes organising, otherwise they won't enjoy it.

- **Scoreboards or progress charts:** Create a simple scoreboard or progress chart and communicate progress on it weekly. People love seeing numbers / results / progress, and talking about it weekly keeps up the healthy competition.
- **Weekly check-ins:** Have a short weekly call or catch up where people's wins and progress are shared and celebrated.
- **Prizes and celebrations:** Don't let the challenge fizzle out at the end. Do something to mark the end of the challenge and celebrate the winners and best efforts. You'll be amazed at how motivated your people will be by simple prizes.

Here are some ideas for challenges for you. If you have two ideas for each category, you have two years of challenges planned:

- **Movement:** step challenge, squat flexibility challenge
- **Sleep:** no screens after 7pm challenge; no-screen activity challenge (points for evening activities that aren't screen-based, such as reading, board games)
- **Nutrition:** healthy breakfast challenge, five fruit and veg challenge
- **Mind:** volunteer / do good challenge, gratitude challenge

Summary

Improving health can be straightforward. Many struggle due to societal norms and an environment in the UK that doesn't support health. Addressing health concerns is simpler than many think. As a business owner, recognising this provides you with an opportunity to make a difference. Unlike others bogged down by health issues, you view these challenges as chances for improvement. Your team look up to you and the other leaders in your business. By prioritising health alongside work, you set a powerful example.

Implementing a few strategies from this chapter can significantly impact your team. Expertise in health isn't a prerequisite, but a basic understanding can enhance both your own life and your influence on others. While physical health often takes precedence, starting with mental health can create better long-term results. The following chapter explains why this approach is beneficial.

EIGHT
Mental Health

For most of humanity's time on this planet, we were hunter-gatherers. We didn't worry then about our mental health. Today, life couldn't be more different. In the developed world, we have lifestyles that enable a level of comfort and luxury previous generations would not have been able to comprehend. Yet with these gifts come challenges. One of the challenges that has become more prevalent recently, is poor mental health.

Dealing with your own mental health can feel burdensome at times, so feeling responsible for the mental health of others can really pack the load of responsibility on your shoulders. As if the challenges of starting and growing a business weren't enough already, the business owners of today have the added requirement of supporting the mental health of their people. The irony is that this can create a huge amount of stress for business owners, leaders and managers.

But here is the good news. You don't need a degree in psychiatry to create an environment that is conducive to good mental health. Although you will never be able to solve all issues, treat mental illness or guarantee good mental health, with a little understanding and some basic systems you can do a fantastic job of supporting people in looking after their mental health, which benefits both them and your business.

Unintentionally, many business cultures have a more negative than positive impact on people's overall mental health. By the end of this chapter, you will understand why this is and exactly how to change it in your own business. It's important to caveat here that I am not a mental health professional, and I'm not talking about curing people of diagnosed conditions. I'm simply sharing with you what I know works when it comes to promoting good mental health in business. These insights have been gained through:

- My own experience of business ownership and mental health
- My work with psychologists and mentors
- Real-life experiences of working with other business owners and professionals

My recommendations are based on two fundamental beliefs:

1. Prevention is better than cure.
2. Your business is perfectly positioned to positively impact the mental health of your employees.

In this chapter, I share the systems, insights and techniques that have helped me transform my own mental health in relation to business as well as the mental health of hundreds of others. Don't take what I share as gospel. Try it yourself and with your people and, if it works, keep going.

What does mental health mean?

Before we look at how to improve it, let's get clear on what mental health actually means. My experience has taught me that most people use or understand the word 'mental health' in a negative context. For example, if somebody is off work with stress people might say 'Steve has mental health.' This is a problem because 'mental health' is a thing to be measured and it can, of course, be in a good or bad place. As we covered earlier, a person's 'mental health' refers to the condition of their mind. Just as you can have good or poor physical health, you can have good or poor mental health.

As the leader of a business, you know how important it is to think in the medium and long term as well as the short term. If you were to only think short term you might shut your highly successful business down because it had a poor week for sales. It's important to apply the same thinking to mental health. Good mental health is not the constant feeling of happiness, just as a few days of feeling tired and negative is not poor mental health. People are human beings and will experience the inevitable ups and downs of life, and a full spectrum of feelings, thoughts and emotions.

My view of mental health has been shaped by the influences of Western and Eastern philosophy. Had my military service been my only career, I might have formed the belief that good mental health means an ability to be strong and resilient in all circumstances, to not let emotion be a driving factor in your life. But my experience of living in monasteries in Southeast Asia taught me that good mental health meant a deep sense of fulfilment that one finds through being a good person and making positive contributions to the world. My further experiences working with mentors and psychologists have altered that understanding again.

Instead of guiding you through each phase of learning that I went through, I'd like to share with you what I now believe to be a good definition of mental health for business owners and leaders:

> 'One's general feelings and ability to handle difficult situations.'

If a person's feelings are generally positive and they can handle the inevitable difficult situations that life throws at them well, then they have good mental health. When a person's feelings are generally negative and they struggle to handle the hard parts of life, they have poor mental health.

Your business can play a significant role in developing great mental health for the majority of people that work for you. Let's look at how.

Businesses and mental health

The avoidance of pain does not, by default, lead to a happy mind or life. Although no person wants to feel pain, it is an inevitable part of life that can enable learning and shape character. A child does not learn to walk without falling over and hurting themselves. An adult cannot achieve a good level of fitness without pushing themselves and feeling some physical pain. The same is true for mental health. You need to experience levels of stress and challenge to build up mental resilience. In my experience, too little mental stress – or too much mental comfort – will usually lead to what I call 'subtle poor mental health'. This is where a person isn't particularly stressed but they lack a sense of fulfilment in their lives. This feeling is usually self-medicated with distractions such as phone scrolling, spending money, thrill seeking, drinking alcohol, casual use of drugs and so on.

Of course, some of these activities can form part of a healthy life but, all too often, if people are honest, they are used as a distraction from what's going on in the mind, such as a yearning for more. This form of 'subtle poor mental health' is less extreme than the poor mental health that can result from excessive stress, but much more common.

The impact of excessive stress can be a lot more potent. My experiences of working with addicts and owning a business opened my eyes to this. People who have had five or more Adverse Childhood Experiences are ten times more likely to become substance abusers, and up to 75% of people who have experienced serious trauma have reported alcohol abuse.[33] These are people who have had no control over what's happened to them and carry around the trauma of past events in their minds, which manifests as stress. As the level of stress is excessive, alcohol or drug use can shift from a weekend distraction to an abusive habit.

Studies show that 72% of entrepreneurs report mental health concerns and 30% have a lifetime history of depression.[34] Unlike the many people who habitually choose excessive comfort, the business owner is future-focused and values-driven, which often causes them immense stress. Before going into business, I had served in the military, completed two tours of Afghanistan and worked twenty-hour shifts on deep sea fishing boats. But until I opened my first business, I had never experienced poor health from excessive stress. When you're highly motivated by your goals there is a risk of an unhealthy amount of self-imposed stress.

For good mental health, we require a healthy amount of stress. Not enough to overwhelm, but not too little that we can't find fulfilment. We have already learned how your business can provide meaningful long-term goals that give people a reason to stretch themselves. We have also covered how to use systems that break your vision down into goals that push people without being overwhelming or excessively stressful. Combine this with the employee happiness data you collect and the employee PDP process, and you already have in place the systems that can build a culture of great mental health.

It's also worth considering that your business might be the *only* vehicle that has a financial incentive to support the good mental health of your people. When they are mentally fit and healthy, they do better work for your company and help it to grow. When they have poor mental health, they can't perform optimally and are more likely to take short- and long-term sickness absence.

Whereas many businesses see employee mental health as a challenge, Better Happy businesses view it as an opportunity. The world in which we live is increasingly supportive of poor mental health because, unfortunately, poor mental health is profitable. Certain activities, when done to excess, contribute to poor mental health – but they also make a lot of money, so they aren't going away. I'm thinking, for example, of:

- Gaming
- Phone scrolling
- Watching TV
- Eating ultra-processed foods

Your business should be a place where people are supported and encouraged to thrive mentally, not just a place where steps are taken to prevent or respond to poor mental health. Your business and every team within it has goals for people to stretch towards, you need to ensure they are supported to do this, so that they can flourish and not struggle.

Why people struggle and how to navigate it

Regardless of all the great systems you've put in place, people in your business will still struggle with their mental health. Why? Because it's part of the human condition. There are so many factors at play, from genetics to life experiences, that you can never eradicate the risk or reality of poor mental health. But you can transform a lot of lives and build a culture that people love to work in by ensuring that you and your people leaders have a basic understanding of:

- How the mind works
- Why it does the things it does
- How to best navigate challenges

When your people feel like they can make consistent progress towards goals (both personal and business goals) in a way that is aligned with their own core values, they will feel good about themselves. It's important, therefore, that you and your leaders / managers make that happen. But why can't it just happen on autopilot?

Homo sapiens have been on the planet for an estimated 2–300,000 years. For 95% of that time we were hunter-gatherers, and the human mind evolved to create behaviours that supported survival of the species. These included:

- Regularly comparing oneself to others – to ensure we fitted into the tribe and were not kicked out, which could have meant death.
- Spotting the negative – anything unusual could have been fatal, so it made sense to home in on anything that was different or felt wrong.

- Fear of conflict – any conflict could be deadly and was therefore avoided or responded to with aggression.
- Fear of the new – anything unknown could carry a risk of death, so it was better to avoid it and stick to what was familiar.
- Fear of judgement – anything that could bring disapproval could result in expulsion from the tribe, so it was better to stay quiet and fit in.
- Greed – food and supplies were hard to come by so it was best to hoard them when available.[35]

For you and your people, all of this means that moving towards goals and doing the right thing isn't as straightforward as you might hope. The evolutionary overhang in the human mind can subconsciously override our conscious thoughts and intentions, leading us to engage in behaviours that aren't congruent with who we want to be. This leads to dissipation of self-worth and poor mental health. The easy option when this happens is to abandon all goals and jump straight back into that comfort zone. What's actually happening here is the more primitive part of the mind is winning and the person is back to the slow burn of subtle poor mental health.

As you have been implementing what you've learned in this book, you will realise that this is no longer an option in your business. In a Better Happy business, people are always growing, personally and professionally. The achievement of the goal is less important than the development of the person in the pursuit of that goal. Unachieved goals are an inevitable part of being a happy, growth-minded person. But a person who gives up or doesn't develop is one who is allowing that primitive part of their mind to override the goal- and values-driven part of their mind. Your job (or the job of their line manager) is to help this person discover why this is happening and, if possible, help them navigate past it.

At this point, it's worth mentioning again that you are not likely to be a qualified health professional and I am not suggesting that you should try to be. All you can do is facilitate conversations to help people identify potential unconscious mental barriers that are hindering their progress. Sometimes the identification of these barriers alone is enough to help the person progress; sometimes, when the barriers are persistent, the person will need to seek professional help.

Let's now look at a simple tool that you and your managers can use to help yourselves and your colleagues thrive mentally.

The ACT Matrix

When I returned to the UK from Southeast Asia and began working with other businesses, I wanted to share what I had learned in the monasteries and how it had transformed my mental health. It helped me quit drinking, be comfortable in my own company and find inner peace. But meditation and Buddhist philosophy was deemed too 'woo woo' for mass audiences in businesses.

A few years later, after experiencing burnout I worked with a psychologist who introduced me to ACT – Acceptance Commitment Training, or Therapy – and I knew instantly that it would not only help me but could help businesses and professionals too.

The method was made famous through the book *The Happiness Trap* by Russ Harris,[36] and it adds a Western lens of practicality to the Eastern philosophy I had learned. ACT teaches you to identify your values in life and then recognise the unhelpful thoughts or feelings that prevent you from living in a way that is aligned to those values. When I implemented this process in my own life and saw its effects, I learned that a person's values are the key to their mental wellbeing. When you are aligned with your values, regardless of what's happening around you, you feel a level of contentment; when you are not aligned, even if you have experienced wild success, you will feel unhappy.

To utilise this approach in your business to support your employees, all you have to do is help your people identify what their values are, and to recognise the thoughts or feelings that are preventing them from being aligned to those values. The ACT Matrix makes doing this easy.

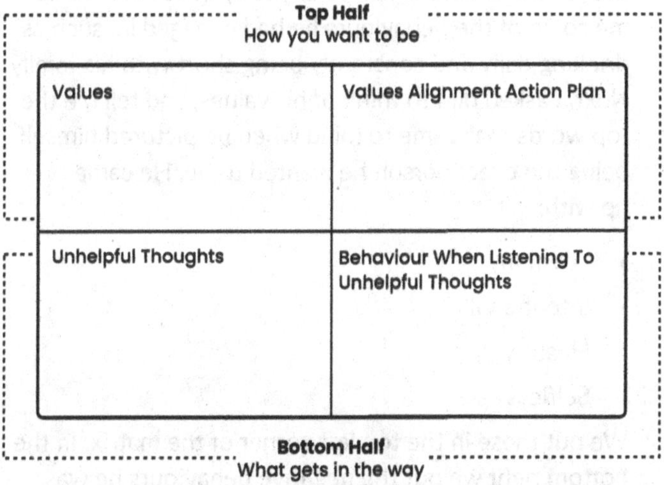

To help you understand how the tool works, I'll share with you a real-life (but anonymised) example.

MENTAL HEALTH DEEP DIVE: Rob

Rob was leading the development of the new branch of a company I was working with. Rob and I had a one-to-one where the aim was to get clear on the goals for that year. Very quickly, it became apparent that the main issue to address was Rob's mental health. Rob was struggling with the weight of responsibility of the business and had fallen into a vicious cycle of destructive behaviour that he had kept concealed from everyone else. I explained to him that there was no point in trying to address things with the branch until we had addressed things with him.

We identified that Rob was stressed by the demands of the job but hadn't talked to anybody about it. He told me some of the behaviours he had engaged in, such as drinking daily and constantly being short with his family. Next, I asked him to think of his values, and tell me the top words that came to mind when he pictured himself being the exact person he wanted to be. He came up with:

- I own my sh*t
- Intentional
- Healthy
- Selfless

We put these in the top left corner of the matrix. In the bottom right we put the negative behaviours he was engaging in, such as excessive drinking, not spending time with his kids, being short with people and bottling up his feelings. When you do this exercise with someone who is struggling, you will notice that some of their actions are in stark contrast to their values.

I then asked Rob what feelings were getting in the way of him being who he wanted to be. He identified a fear of conflict and embarrassment that he didn't have all the answers. As we wrote these things down, Rob started to realise how daft these thoughts were. This is the power of putting things down on paper – most of us respond to these kinds of thoughts on autopilot without understanding how unhelpful or illogical they are. After writing down these thoughts, Rob already had a clear idea of what he needed to do to get more aligned to his values. Here's what he came up with:

- Book a chat with X from the business to share what I'm struggling with and build a better plan or get more help.
- Talk to my partner and plan a monthly activity away with her and the kids.
- Give myself time and permission to be active again and have at least three hours a week 'me' time.
- Limit drinking to weekends only.

You can guide people to find steps to improve but it's important that it's them who ultimately decides on the plan, instead of just writing down your good ideas. Sometimes the problems will be deep-rooted and neither of you will know the next steps. In these situations, it's best to signpost the person to professional support. Your job isn't to fix the issues but to facilitate the conversation that uncovers them – and you'll be amazed at the transformative impact just having that conversation can have on someone's life.

After the session, I got a 'thank you' message from Rob but then I didn't hear from him again until our next appointment two months later, when he proudly told me he hadn't had a single drink since we last met. He didn't realise how much of the stress he felt came from work and how that stress manifested as destructive behaviours. He told me the first thing he did was 'own his sh*t' and go and speak with his boss. He was nervous but his boss was totally supportive and agreed to hire someone else and help him more with the project. That horror story he'd dreamed up of what would happen if he shared that he was struggling, simply wasn't true. The evolutionary part of his mind had taken over and all Rob had to do was recognise that, get clear on his values and take action.

Imagine if he hadn't taken the time to do that activity. He would still be engaging in destructive behaviour that made him hate himself because some subconscious part of his mind had told him that if he shared his lack of confidence, he'd lose his job. Most of the barriers to you and your people being the happiest versions of yourselves are inaccurate, subconscious thoughts with no grounding in reality.

There are other techniques for addressing this but there is nothing simpler or more practical and impactful than the ACT Matrix. Next time you are struggling with a situation, or somebody shares with you that they are, work through it this way. It's one of the most powerful exercises in this book.

Summary

Although you likely didn't start your business to support people with their mental health, it can be one of its unexpected joys. Some business owners have high empathy and love the people side of things, whereas others are more introverted and prefer the vision/systems aspects. Whichever type of owner you are, you want healthy, happy people in your business and you want people to love working for you. The learnings from Part Two enabled you to build a growth-minded and motivating environment. One of the inevitable challenges of nurturing such an environment is that, as you push yourself and others, people may struggle with stress. This isn't because stress is bad but because, as society has become increasingly comfortable, people just aren't used to it. With the insights and tools I have shared with you in this chapter, you can support yourself and others to overcome or avoid stress-related struggles for improved mental health. In the next chapter, we'll look at how you can achieve the same for physical health.

NINE
Physical Health

Just like the mind, the body hasn't yet evolved to naturally thrive in the modern environment. The extreme contrasts between the lifestyle of the hunter-gatherer and that of the modern human give rise to challenges but also opportunities for physical health.

With a basic understanding of the body and some simple systems, people can enjoy great levels of physical health in the modern world. This is good news for businesses. Poor physical health is a double-edged sword for business owners and leaders. First, business owners feel guilty because the work they give their employees may itself be having a negative impact on their physical health. The office worker sits for eight plus hours a day; the factory worker lifts heavy boxes over and over. Both are at risk of bad backs, necks, shoulders, etc. Second, poor physical health has a financial impact on a business. The costs are wide ranging, from lost productivity to covering sickness absence. In 2022/23, 35.2 million working days were lost due to self-reported work-related ill health or injury, with an estimated annual cost of £20.7 billion.[37]

When you change your thinking, you change your reality. From my experience, many people believe you can't be healthy alongside a job unless you are health-obsessed. This belief is limiting and incorrect. In this chapter, I'll discuss three key ideas that will lay the foundations for great levels of physical health in your business and in your own life:

- Modern life makes it easier to be healthy than ever before.
- Being healthy isn't difficult or complicated.
- Your business is the perfect vehicle for creating good physical health.

By grasping these concepts, you will change your thinking around health and see this manifest in your own life and business. Whereas most other businesses will battle with the costs of sickness, you will reap the benefits of great physical health. You will feel a sense of pride knowing that your employees are actively improving their health by working for you. Your employees will be blown away by the value you place on their wellbeing, generating levels of loyalty and engagement other businesses can only dream of.

What is physical health?

Although there is still much suffering in the world, quality of life has generally improved. Although we can be blinded by the negativity and issues that still exist, the reality is that the improvements we have made and continue to make are incredible. For example:

- The number of those living in extreme poverty has dropped from 80% of the world in 1820 to less than 10% in 2019.
- Global literacy rates have risen from 10% in 1820 to 87% today.
- Child mortality rates have dropped from 47% in 1800 to 4% in 2021.[38]

We are highly driven to remove the pains of life and have proven remarkably efficient at doing so. Just look at how technology has enabled us to remove much of the physical labour that historically was required for our survival and growth. This is a step forward but brings with it a new challenge. For the first time in history, people do not need to be physically healthy in order to survive and meet their basic needs. Physical health has gone from being a non-negotiable byproduct of staying alive to a 'nice to have' that must be achieved through design and deliberate effort.

In this new context where physical health and fitness requires a conscious decision, it's important that you know what physical health is. The definition we used earlier is, 'The condition of the body and the degree to which it is free from illness, or the state of being well.'

What you want to achieve in your own life and support your employees to achieve in theirs is not just being free from illness but the state of being *well*. But what does 'being well' mean? For me, being well means:

- Having good energy levels
- Being free from pain
- Feeling strong
- Being independent and confident in one's physicality

You can be like most people and businesses where the aim is to not be sick, or not be in pain, or not be overweight. Or you can be different and aim to be healthy. To be *well*. My definition above provides clarity on what that might look like.

The lowest common denominator of health

Every person perceives health differently. Even in the medical world, there are lots of different ways to measure health that contradict each other and sometimes make no sense. When I signed up for the army I was told I had to lose half a stone because my body mass index (BMI) placed me in the obese category. The BMI measurement tool is a chart that uses your height and weight to give a score. Although the chart said I was obese, I was heavy because I lifted a lot of weights. My body fat was very low, at 15%, and I went on to be awarded 'fittest recruit' in basic training. BMI is still widely used as a gauge of health by the NHS today.

Whenever I'm covering physical health with a new business or team, I like to run an experiment. I first ask everyone in the room to raise their hands if they are genuinely interested in physical fitness – for example, dedicating at least a few hours a week to training in the gym, or playing a sport, with the intended outcome of increased performance or changed physical appearance. Typically, 30% of the room raise their hands. Then I ask how many people are genuinely interested in health. Here I mean having good energy levels, being pain free and increasing their chances of living a healthy life for as long as possible. Always, 100% of the room put their hands up. Not everybody in your business wants to be fit, but everyone wants to be healthy. This is why corporate gym memberships, if the goal is to improve employee health, are a waste of money. Only the 30% who are interested in fitness (and so are likely already healthy) will use them. You'll have a much wider impact – and higher ROI – by focusing on communicating and encouraging the basics of good health.

Health is easier than fitness

Though as we've already learned, it's never been easier to be unhealthy, it's also never been easier to be healthy. You have access to fantastic training and nutrition programmes for free online. Food from around the world can be delivered to your doorstep. Most people in the UK live less than twenty minutes away from a gym with high-quality equipment. Most smartphones have apps that can help you monitor your sleep and count your daily steps. Our jobs are less physically demanding and average working patterns are forty hours a week. This leaves seventy-two weekly hours awake (assuming eight hours' sleep per night) or ten hours daily of non-working hours. Yes, people have children, commutes and other commitments, but the reality is that time is rarely a genuine barrier to good health. Yet the majority of people still struggle. This is because people:

- Aren't sure what to do
- Don't believe in themselves

- Want to skip the boring basics and find quick fixes

One way to address this is to be clear on the difference between health and fitness. I share the following pyramid with people we train and it's always an 'Aha' moment.

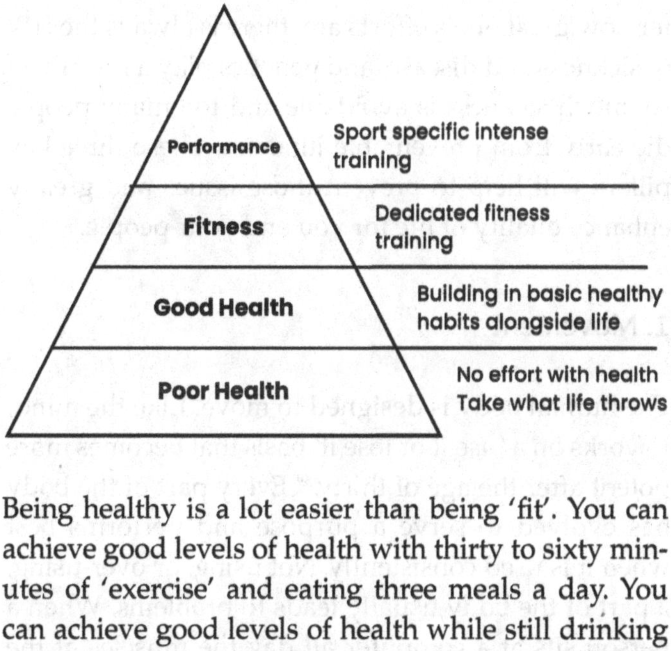

Being healthy is a lot easier than being 'fit'. You can achieve good levels of health with thirty to sixty minutes of 'exercise' and eating three meals a day. You can achieve good levels of health while still drinking alcohol, eating chocolate and sitting down for eight hours a day. You don't have to step foot in a gym or run anywhere if you don't want to. You can hate fitness and still enjoy great health. The sooner you help your people realise this, the better. You just need to show them that they are capable. Achieving good health isn't about some huge life shift or finding the right hack; it's about building simple habits into your daily life across three main areas.

The three key pillars of physical health

Good physical health is the outcome of good habits across three key pillars – and a serving of luck. No matter how great one's efforts are, there is always the risk of sickness and disease, and genetics play a role. Even so, much sickness is avoidable and too many people die early from preventable illnesses. These three key pillars will help to prevent those issues and greatly enhance quality of life for you and your people.

1. Movement

The human body is designed to move. Like the mind, it works on a 'use it or lose it' basis that becomes more potent after the age of thirty.[39] Every part of the body has evolved to serve a purpose and performs best when it is used consistently. Not using, or over-using, a part of the body usually leads to problems. When a person sits at a computer all day the muscles at the front of their shoulders become tight, the muscles at the back of their shoulders become lengthened and weak, and this leads to neck pain. When people don't get their heart rate up regularly, their heart and lungs weaken. When bones aren't stressed through exercise they can weaken, leading to osteoporosis.

The good news is you don't need to move all day to satisfy the 'use it or lose it' principle. A little bit of effort provides a huge benefit. Consider bodybuilders. They train for a few hours a day but they only move weights for around 10% of that time, the rest of the session is spent on recovery. And we're not talking about bodybuilding here. It doesn't take long at all to keep your joints, muscles and bones healthy.

When it comes to movement and health, there are three areas you need to consider:

1. Heart and lung health – commonly known as CV (cardiovascular) or CR (cardiorespiratory)
2. Bone and muscle health
3. Postural (joint) health

Giving basic attention to all three of these areas can help to offset many preventable health issues common in the modern world, such as joint pain and osteoporosis. Bone and postural health can be looked after through a simple daily mobility routine that takes no longer than ten minutes. Adding weight to the movements once you can perform them pain-free will lead to further benefits.

MOBILITY DEEP DIVE: Lucy's story

Lucy works at an accountancy firm. We trained her team on physical health and introduced the mobility routine. Lucy was in her fifties and living with a lot of stiffness and joint pain. She thought this was just part of getting older and that there was nothing she could do about it. I advised her to make the mobility routine a non-negotiable part of her day and not to force it. Six months later, Lucy, with a beaming smile on her face, told me that not only was she still doing her mobility routine daily, but that she had gone from struggling to bouncing out of bed every morning.

To implement this into the culture of your business, print off the mobility routine we use from the link below, and run a four-week mobility challenge. Part of the routine involves getting a current mobility score; this adds a level of excitement when run as a challenge, because everyone wants to get to the next level. Some of our clients put mobility stations in their offices, with wall-mounted posters that guide people through the daily routine. It takes them less than ten minutes and becomes a normal part of the day.

To help people with their heart and lung health, you simply have to find ways to encourage people to move more. A simple but effective way to do this is to run a step challenge, where you make a certain number of steps a day non-negotiable and encourage people to increase from their baseline. This doesn't have to involve public accountability – it's about encouraging and supporting people, not shaming them. And of course, consider that not all employees will be able-bodied and some may have hidden disabilities.

There is a mobility routine available for you at www.betterhappybusinessclub.com/book-bonus.

2. Nutrition

Humans evolved in a context of food scarcity. The only foods that were available to us were those that our landscape and immediate environment provided – vegetables, fruits, nuts, seeds, meat and fish. Sourcing enough food to survive was the daily focus for most of our existence. Then, approximately 10,000 years ago, we established agricultural practices. This enabled us to grow as a species, which created a new problem… we had a lot of people but not enough readily available food. The solution came in the form of advanced food preservation and processing. Today, for the majority of us, a lack of food is not something we worry about. The new problem is eating too much, which has caused high levels of obesity. Alongside 'fitness', nutrition is an important component of health.

Exactly what good nutrition looks like, what the perfect diet is, whether we should be vegetarian, vegan or carnivorous, are widely debated. But there are some simple principles you can follow and know that you've got the basics of good nutrition down:

1. Regularly consuming too many calories is bad for you.
2. Eating and drinking processed foods makes it easy to consume too many calories.
3. Eating mainly whole unprocessed foods is generally good for you.

From experience, I know that the most common nutrition-related issue with hard-working professionals is they don't eat enough in the day. They skip breakfast, buy something quick for lunch then get home hungry at the end of the day. This hunger leads to overeating not long before bed and, the next day, the cycle starts over. Most professionals could transform their nutrition and health by incorporating a healthy breakfast and lunch into their day. A healthy meal should include a source of protein, healthy fats and fruit or veg.

NUTRITION DEEP DIVE: Pete's story

Pete is a senior sales trainer at a hospitality business we work with. He had tried to lose weight for years and was surprised when I told him that he was struggling to do so because he didn't eat enough in the day. He committed to eating a breakfast of natural yoghurt, a good-quality granola and fruit. As he didn't have time to do this at home, he had it in the office. When I saw Pete a few months later he was happy to tell me about two things that had happened. First, he'd lost 10lbs without changing anything other than breakfast. He attributed this to the fact that he wasn't 'kicking the door of the shop down' at lunch to buy a meal deal with all the extras. He was making better choices because he wasn't starving. Second, his team had noticed his new breakfast habit, quizzed him on it and then adopted it themselves. Don't underestimate the impact your actions can have on others.

Healthy breakfast and lunch challenges are by far the most impactful way to incorporate better nutrition into your business. If you skip breakfast then rush to fit in a processed lunch, your people will see this and will likely do the same.

3. Sleep

Hunter-gatherers didn't have alarm clocks. Until recently, we largely followed natural sleep patterns dictated by hormones and sunlight. Documented major changes to this came with the industrial revolution.[40] Industry required shift working, which required regulated sleep patterns manipulated by the factory bell/whistle. Lack of sleep is linked to many chronic health problems including heart disease, obesity and depression.[41] Sleep is the most important of the three pillars, but I always leave it until last when working with people because I've found that habits tend to improve once good movement and nutrition habits are in place.

Many people in the modern world struggle with sleep, often due to a combination of low levels of physical activity, poor diet, high stress and, last but not least... the advent of readily accessible digital media. Spending the evening watching screens that emit blue light tricks the body into thinking it is still daytime. This can suppress the release of the sleep hormone, melatonin, making it difficult to fall asleep. That's why when you read a book in bed you struggle to get through ten pages but if you scroll on your phone you can easily stay awake for two hours. Good sleep requires planning and good evening habits.

Bringing sleep challenges into the workplace is less exciting, for obvious reasons, but you can still bring an element of fun to it. We have found the following challenges work well:

- Reading thirty pages a night challenge (to replace phone scrolling)
- No phones or screens after 7pm
- In bed by XX

Other tips for good sleep hygiene are to change all of the lightbulbs in your house to low lumen bulbs, building sleep mode into your phone settings and discovering your unique 'sleep type' – also known as a chronotype. An attendee on one of our courses was upset with himself for not spending quality time with his kids in the evening. Instead, he would just sit on his phone. He downloaded an app that made his phone black and white and minimised its usability after a set time. This meant he was not tempted by his phone, spent more and better time with his kids and consistently got to sleep over an hour earlier without a struggle.

Summary

Good health is good for business. While most people look for that one magical thing that will transform their health easily, there's only one way to do it: good basic habits. Being healthy is a generalist, not specialist activity. You don't need to have the world's best diet or be able to run a marathon. You don't need to intermittently fast, do CrossFit or meditate every day. Sure, all of these things can be great but, to the majority of people who just want to be healthy and get on with their lives, they are unnecessary. We're all human. Life gets busy, we get distracted and we let important habits slip. We put ourselves last and let the problems of life take priority. The problem is… there are always more problems.

By doing the following, your business will be the entity in your employees' lives that helps them look after their health:

- Make health a priority in your business
- Ensure that you and your leadership team model the right behaviours
- Run simple health challenges throughout the year

Just think about the impact these simple actions will have on you, your people and your business. There's every reason to do them and no good reason not to.

Conclusion

It's my hope that after reading this book you now see your life and business in a different light. You're a born leader, naturally driven to make things happen. But as we've covered, without the right structure around you, your drive can end up making life difficult. You put not only yourself at risk of poor health and burnout but those within your business too. It's a sad reality that most business owners feel stuck in their businesses and most businesses aren't great places to work. Throughout this book we have covered why that happens and why now is the perfect time to do something about it so that you, your people and your business can not just survive but *thrive*.

The SELPH method provides you with a framework for aligning your life, business and teams. By following it you can avoid the most common issues holding businesses back and making them unenjoyable places to work. Business owners are notoriously future-focused and overly optimistic. This means we often bite off more than we can chew, take on too much and try to move at 100 miles per hour. Working within the SELPH framework enables you to offset the potential negatives of those traits and capitalise on the positives.

If there's one thing that I've learned over the past few years, it's that businesses don't become ineffective and stressful because people don't care. It's the opposite. They become ineffective and stressful because people care so much. They care about the business and they care about each other. They want to get results but they don't want to upset or offend the other people involved. Left unchecked, this leads to poor collaboration, built-up resentments and overwork. The SELPH method enables you to systematically overcome those common issues so that you can all get rowing quicker and in the same direction.

When people are inspired by their work and working collaboratively with others, health and happiness levels shoot up. If you want to grow your business, create a great, healthy culture for your employees and improve your own life.

I have no doubt you're going to be excited to start implementing the SELPH method today, but perhaps you might also feel overwhelmed at the sheer volume of things to do. I want to reassure you that implementing the lessons of this book will be transformative for your business. But it takes time. To make this process easier, I have the following resources for you:

- **The Better Happy scorecard:** Completing this short free scorecard will give you clarity on how you are performing against the SELPH model right now. Using this data, you can identify the highest impact areas to focus on first. You can take the quiz as many times as you like and track your progress. It's available via the free resources link.
- **Free resources:** We have a library of free resources to accompany this book available via the free resources link at www.betterhappybusinessclub.com/book-bonus. Here you'll find everything you need to start making dramatic changes in each component of the SELPH method and your business.

Work with Better Happy

Get better results, faster with more enjoyment by partnering with Better Happy. We have a variety of workshops, programmes and partnerships that we run every year. You can find out more about all of our offers via the following links:

Small businesses: www.betterhappybusinessclub.com

Medium and large businesses: www.betterhappy.co.uk

Get investment in your small business:
www.mikejones.live

Remember, life and businesses are better happy.

Notes

1 Simply Business, 'Over half of small business owners have experienced poor mental health over the past 12 months' (Simply Business, 15 May 2023) www.simplybusiness.co.uk/about-us/press-releases/mind-your-business-launch, accessed March 2024

2 T Brower, 'Managers have major impact on mental health: How to lead for wellbeing', Forbes (29 January 2023) www.forbes.com/sites/tracybrower/2023/01/29/managers-have-major-impact-on-mental-health-how-to-lead-for-wellbeing, accessed March 2024

3 Gallup, 'State of the Global Workplace: 2023 Report' (Gallup, 2023) www.gallup.com/workplace/349484/state-of-the-global-workplace.aspx, accessed March 2024

4 T Mello, *Elevate: Build a business where everybody wins* (Mark Victor Hansen Library, 2023)
5 C Steinhorst, 'Why Your Workforce Is Bored Out Of Their Minds' (*Forbes*, 28 January 2020) www.forbes.com/sites/curtsteinhorst/2020/01/28/why-your-workforce-is-bored-out-of-their-minds/?sh=4ff2d01d208d, accessed 24 April 2024
6 C Baker, 'Obesity statistics' (House of Commons Library, 12 January 2023) https://commonslibrary.parliament.uk/research-briefings/sn03336, accessed March 2024
7 BBC News, 'Job vacancies outpace unemployment for first time' (BBC News, 17 May 2022) www.bbc.co.uk/news/uk-61475720, accessed March 2024
8 G Orwell, *The Road to Wigan Pier* (Penguin Classics, 2001)
9 J Rohn, *The Art of Exceptional Living* (Simon & Schuster Audio, 2008)
10 Oxford English Dictionary, 'Strategy' (OED, nd) www.oed.com/dictionary/strategy_n?tab=factsheet#20537476, accessed March 2024
11 T Lemmon, 'Two thirds of SMEs still don't have a business plan' (Accountancy Age, 3 September 202), www.accountancyage.com/2020/09/03/two-thirds-of-smes-still-dont-have-a-business-plan, accessed March 2024
12 Oxfam, 'Vision, mission and beliefs', https://oxfamapps.org/cymru/vision-mission-and-beliefs, accessed April 2024

13 IKEA, 'The IKEA vision and values', www.ikea.com/gb/en/this-is-ikea/about-us/the-ikea-vision-and-values-pub9aa779d0, accessed March 2024
14 Better Happy, 'Our Vision', https://betterhappy.co.uk/about, accessed April 2024
15 'Amazon Mission, Vision & Values', www.comparably.com/companies/amazon/mission, accessed May 2024
16 ChangesUK are gone now as a company, but this was the mission statement that we helped them write.
17 Amazon, 'Who we are', www.aboutamazon.co.uk/who-we-are, accessed March 2024
18 IKEA, 'IKEA culture and values', www.ikea.com/global/en/our-business/how-we-work/ikea-culture-and-values, accessed March 2024
19 Dent, 'Our Values', www.dent.global/about-us, accessed April 2024
20 Gallup, 'State of the Global Workplace: 2023 Report' (Gallup, 2023) www.gallup.com/workplace/349484/state-of-the-global-workplace.aspx, accessed March 2024
21 M Tenney, 'The link between employee engagement and business performance' (Business Leadership Today, nd) https://businessleadershiptoday.com/the-link-between-employee-engagement-and-business-performance, accessed March 2024
22 S Mcleod, 'Maslow's Hierarchy of Needs' (Simply Psychology, 24 January 2024)

www.simplypsychology.org/maslow.html, accessed March 2024
23 The hierarchy of human needs, adapted from Maslow's Hierarchy of Needs, AH Maslow, 'A theory of human motivation', *Psychological Review*, 50/4 (1943), 370-396, https://doi.org/10.1037/h0054346
24 P Lencioni, *The Five Dysfunctions of a Team* (John Wiley & Sons, 2002)
25 Ciphr, 'Unpaid overtime statistics' (Ciphr, 2023) www.ciphr.com/unpaid-overtime-statistics-2023, accessed March 2024
26 The Wellbeing Project, 'The causes of middle manager burnout' (The Wellbeing Project, 26 June 2023) https://thewellbeingproject.co.uk/insight/the-causes-of-middle-manager-burnout, accessed March 2024
27 Simply Business, 'Over half of small business owners have experienced poor mental health over the past 12 months' (Simply Business, 15 May 2023) www.simplybusiness.co.uk/about-us/press-releases/mind-your-business-launch, accessed March 2024
28 Cambridge Dictionary, 'Performance', https://dictionary.cambridge.org/dictionary/english/performance, accessed March 2024
29 Cambridge Dictionary, 'Mental health', https://dictionary.cambridge.org/dictionary/english/health, accessed March 2024
30 UK Government, 'The Health and Safety at Work Act 1974', www.hse.gov.uk/legislation/hswa.htm, accessed March 2024

31 UK Government, 'The Statutory Sick Pay Up-rating (No. 2) Order 1983, www.legislation.gov.uk/uksi/1983/1947/contents/made, accessed March 2024
32 The Office for National Statistics, 'Avoidable mortality in the UK: 2019' (ONS, 26 February 2021) www.ons.gov.uk/peoplepopulationandcommunity/healthandsocialcare/causesofdeath/bulletins/avoidablemortalityinenglandandwales/2019, accessed March 2024
33 D McMahon, 'When trauma slips into addiction' (The Imprint, 17 December 2018) https://imprintnews.org/child-trauma-2/when-trauma-slips-into-addiction/32462, accessed March 2024
34 B Lee, '72% of entrepreneurs suffer from mental health issues. Here's why – and what to do about it' (Minutes, 2021) https://minutes.co/72-of-entrepreneurs-suffer-from-mental-health-issues-heres-why-and-what-to-do-about-it, accessed March 2024
35 Dr R Harris, 'The Happiness Trap: Evolution of the Human Mind' (YouTube, 26 September 2017) www.youtube.com/watch?v=kv6HkipQcfA, accessed April 2024
36 R Harris, *The Happiness Trap: Stop struggling, start living* (Robinson, 2022)
37 Health and Safety Executive, 'Summary statistics for Great Britain 2023' (HSE, 2023) www.hse.gov.uk/statistics/overview.htm, accessed March 2024

38 M Roser, 'The short history of global living conditions and why it matters that we know it' (Our World in Data, 14 December 2016) https://ourworldindata.org/a-history-of-global-living-conditions, accessed March 2024
39 Harvard Health, 'Preserve your muscle mass' (Harvard Health Publishing, 19 February 2016) www.health.harvard.edu/staying-healthy/preserve-your-muscle-mass, accessed March 2024
40 LV Anderson, 'Down With Alarm Clocks!' (The Drift, 25 November 2015) https://slate.com/human-interest/2015/11/down-with-alarm-clocks-they-are-a-capitalist-trap.html, accessed 24 April 2024
41 National Heart, Lung and Blood Institute, 'What are sleep deprivation and deficiency?', www.nhlbi.nih.gov/health/sleep-deprivation, accessed March 2024

Acknowledgements

I'd like to thank and dedicate this book to my partner Laura who constantly supports and pushes me to achieve my dreams. When my confidence or energy wanes she never fails to prop me back up. She puts zero pressure on me and 100% support. What more can you ask for?

I would also like to thank every client we've worked with from 2020 to date. You put your trust in me and that's enabled us to not only achieve great things together but pave the path for more impact.

The Author

Mike Jones is the founder of award winning business consultancy Better Happy. Mike's unique insights into health, happiness and high performance are developed from his experiences in the military, living in monasteries and owning businesses. His mission is to enable businesses, owners and employees to thrive – together.

Please do connect with Mike and share about your business, and your wins:

www.linkedin.com/company/betterhappy